Joel Rappoport has made Winston-Salem, North Carolina his home since 1971 where he made a living working as a radio announcer and talk show host for over a decade. He currently works as the Safety and Health Manager and Fire Chief at a local packaging company. His love for motorcycle riding began in the early seventies, and has morphed into a desire to ride endless one thousand mile days. This is his first book.

Hopeless Class

By Joel Rappoport

Grateful acknowledgement is made to Michael Kneebone, the Iron Butt
Association, and The Iron Butt Rally for permission to reprint excerpts
from their materials.

The Iron Butt Rally, 11 days 11,000 miles, World's Toughest
Motorcycle Riders, and The Iron Butt Association, are all trademarks of
the Iron Butt Association and Iron Butt Rally. Used with permission.

Special thanks to Steven Hobart, Vonie Glaves, and Rick Miller for the
use of their photographs. All other photographs are by the author.

Dedication

To my wife Susie.
My one true love.

Acknowledgements

This book would not have been written without the constant support and encouragement of my wife Susie. Not only has she been a relentless supporter of my riding insanity over the past three decades, but she has been my trusted advisor and source of strength in my pursuit of long-distance riding success. From the day that I first asked her if she thought I should submit an entry in the 2007 Iron Butt Rally (her immediate reply was "Go for it!"), to the smile on her face when I finished the 2009 IBR, she has been my rock.

I'm grateful to the long-distance riding community and the willingness to share tips and tales with new riders, and to all of the folks at the Iron Butt Association including Mike Kneebone, Lisa Landry, Tom Austin, David McQueeney, Greg Roberts, Dale Wilson, Jim and Donna Fousek, and a large group of volunteers who organize the chaos into a fun sport. Without the volunteers there would be no Iron Butt Rally. Without Mike Kneebone's willingness to allow me to use artwork, bonus information, and other trademarked material, this book would not be as entertaining.

Part of my learning to cover more miles, in less time, was with the help of stories by Bob Higdon. He authored many of the tales of long-distance riding that caught my attention and stoked my fascination with the sport. His writing style has the ability to scoff at the foolishness of what we do, but at the same time shows a respect bordering on awe for the riders.

Bill Thweatt helped me polish my riding abilities before the 2009 IBR and for that I'll be forever grateful. I succeeded in part because Bill would patiently steer me away from bad habits into successful ones.

Nathan Mende, Dean Graham, Rick Jones, and Jerry Heil all were passionate about riding, the BMW R60, and my success in the IBR. They all contributed mightily to my being able to finish the rally.

Finally, I appreciate the diligent work that my wife put into turning what was a short ride-report about the rally into this book. Her willingness to spend endless hours proofreading and editing has been priceless.

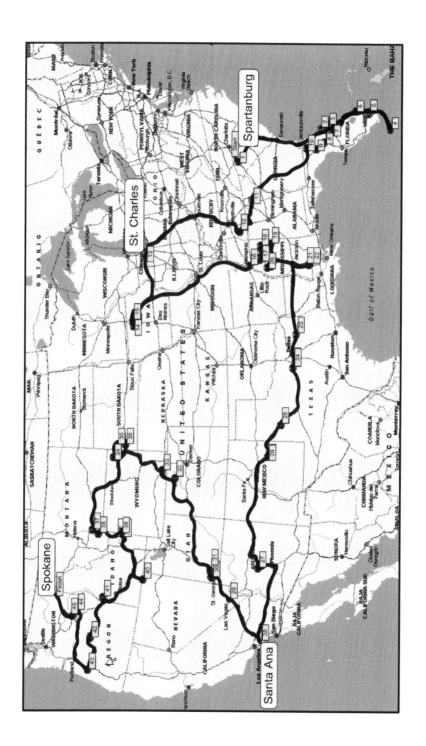

Spartanburg

St. Charles

Spokane

Santa Ana

Prologue

As I became aware of the first faint mental stirring that told me I was waking up, my mind was hurled into a full-blown panic. I didn't hear the normal loud and distinctive wake-up-alarm that I used when I was on a motorcycle rally. I realized that I had overslept, knew that I wasn't where I should be, but didn't have the least idea of where I was.

All that I was certain of was that if I didn't get my act together, and fast, I would blow my chance to get to the final checkpoint of the Iron Butt Motorcycle Rally before it closed. I had invested thousands of dollars and almost a decade of training toward competing in the Iron Butt and oversleeping, even for just a few minutes, would mean disaster. I would be a DNF (did not finish).

It's amazing how much thought can be packed into a short period of time. All of the above took a small fraction of a second. One moment I'm sleeping soundly and then, BOOM, my adrenaline is pumping full-bore, my mind is racing, and I'm doing five things at once.

I was pushing away thoughts of anger that I had somehow not set the alarm correctly. Or maybe I had turned it off and fallen back to sleep. I bolted up out of bed and was looking around the dark room as my mind was vainly attempting to make order out of the unknown. When I stop at a motel during a motorcycle rally I follow a fairly rigid routine. In order to be able to dress quickly I always lay my riding suit, helmet, boots, and gloves on the foot of the motel bed but they weren't there.

To help me get quickly oriented when I wake up I always put a sticky-note on my alarm clock stating the place I stopped, the time I need to get up, and where I'm going to ride next. The clock was bare.

This wasn't good at all! I knew that I was riding the eleven day, eleven thousand mile rally and every second counted. I had stopped for my daily four hour rest and missed my alarm. Another half-second was spent organizing the steps I needed to take to get back on track. I had to get dressed, gather my stuff, check out of the motel, and get riding toward the next rally-bonus RIGHT NOW! I could figure out where I was and how far behind the clock this mistake had put me once I was on the road, but I had to move fast.

As I was looking for my riding suit I could hear a voice talking but I didn't pay it much mind. I first had to work through my list of things that needed to move at light-speed. To add to the confusion, I usually wear hearing aids so I have to pay close attention to what folks say, especially when I don't expect to hear specific words strung together. Without the aids the voice was muffled. However, the voice was also insistent and I gave just a bit of my concentration to it and heard my wife Susie repeating "The rally is over. You're home. The rally is over."

I was still scrambling for my gear when what she said finally clicked. The Iron Butt Rally had ended weeks before. I had successfully finished in fifty-ninth place. I was at home. There were no deadlines, no bonuses, and no problems. I could relax and go back to sleep.

Another portion of a second was spent figuring out if this was actually part of a dream and if I really needed to wake up and get riding, but the pieces fell into place and I relaxed. I sheepishly thanked Susie and then just sat on the edge of the bed.

I was wide awake, in the middle of an adrenaline rush, and knew that I wouldn't be able to go back to sleep for an hour or so. This was not the first time I'd awakened in a blind-charge to ride and it probably wouldn't be the last. I had spent years ordering my mental and physical patterns for the world's toughest motorcycle rally and it would take a while longer to return to normal.

Contents

1 The World's Toughest Motorcycle Riders

Here's the concept. Gather 101 motorcycle riders in Spartanburg, South Carolina, and then turn them loose for an eleven day, eleven thousand mile motorcycle rally across North America. This is a long-distance endurance event and these riders are among the best long-distance riders in the world. They will move about the continent alone, each one following his, or her, own best route to the finish.

For this rally we remove speed from the equation by requiring that the final standings are based on each rider's total number of points gathered by visiting bonus locations scattered across the United States and Canada. The harder it is to travel to and from a bonus, the more points that bonus is worth.

Most of these bonuses are time-sensitive. This may mean that some are only available during daylight hours or work hours or on a certain day. Other bonuses require a walk along the ocean floor to an island or lighthouse so that low tide becomes the deciding time element. Still others require meeting a particular person who will only be available for an hour or two on a specific day.

Stringing a rider's chosen bonuses together usually requires staying in the saddle for eighteen hours or longer each day for eleven straight days. This last ability to ride a motorcycle for endless hours leads to their being referred to as "Iron Butt" riders.

Break this rally into three "legs", each leg ending in a checkpoint where the rider's bonus points will be calculated. The checkpoint window is only open for two hours and penalties start the split-second that the window opens. A tardy rider loses a large number of their hard earned points-per-minute for lateness, and if the rider arrives just one second after the close of the window they are disqualified and their rally is over. Bonus locations for the next leg are given out after the window for the preceding leg ends; therefore the riders don't know where they are going to be riding until the leg actually starts.

None of this sounds too bad until you realize that the organizers of the rally list over one hundred and thirty available bonus locations for each leg and each bonus has a different set of points and requirements. The riders have to spend hours with maps, computer mapping programs, and calculators selecting bonuses for a route that will yield the highest point total, and they do this while the clock is ticking. A good route is never easy to design on day-one and by day-eleven it is an incredibly mind-numbing exercise.

Once the rally-clock starts it never stops. Weather, road conditions, traffic, gloom-of-night, accident, machine failure, rider breakdown, and any of a thousand other conditions don't stop the clock. Participants in the past have ridden through hurricanes, arctic cold, desert heat, and everything in between in order to finish the rally.

As I found when I rode in the 2007 IBR, there are a minimum number of points that are required to be considered a "finisher", so riding from checkpoint to checkpoint won't lead to success. The riders have to be able to keep their wits about them and constantly re-evaluate their routes and the bonuses that they plan to claim under the pressure of this minimum point value.

When the rally is over the participants will have covered around one million miles. The top five riders will carry away a small trophy, while all finishers receive a wall-plaque and a plastic license plate backing plate that reads *Iron Butt*

Rally, 11 Days 11,000 Miles, World's Toughest Motorcycle Rally.

This begs the question: Why would an otherwise sane individual try for years to get a starting place through the lottery-style drawing and then spend thousands of dollars and years of preparation of both motorcycle and rider to participate in the Iron Butt Rally?

It's not for money. There is none. I can't count the number of times that I've described the rally to someone and been asked the question "How much money does the winner get?" When I say that there is no prize money at all, this invariably leads to them asking me "Why would anyone take part in the event?"

I entered because I love long-distance motorcycle riding and the IBR was the ultimate endurance ride. In addition the rally was really a grand adventure, in part because until the rally started the riders had no idea where they may be riding and what they may be required to do. I rode for the enjoyment of safely completing the most difficult motorcycle rally on the planet; and to enjoy the camaraderie of this group of exceedingly atypical folk who love riding endless miles for no other reason than the ride itself.

I also enjoyed the unsettling challenge of completing the rally on a fifty horsepower motorcycle that was a third of a century old, and started the rally with over half a million miles on the odometer. I would be riding the oldest and highest mileage motorcycle in this IBR.

The Iron Butt Rally is organized by the Iron Butt Association (IBA) and by this time I hope that you understand that "Iron Butt" refers to a rider's ability to spend long hours in the saddle day after day.

To join the IBA a rider must complete a basic motorcycle ride of 1,000 miles in 24 hours called a *Saddlesore 1,000*. The rider documents the ride with starting and ending witnesses as well as computer generated receipts gathered along the route from gas stations. The IBA audits the ride to insure that the rider covered the miles that they claim in the hours that are allotted. If all of the paperwork is in order the rider receives a confirmation certificate.

On odd years the Iron Butt Association holds the Iron Butt Rally and riders come from all over the world to share in the adventure. This will be the twenty-fifth anniversary of the IBR. There are countless other long-distance motorcycle rallies held in the United States and other countries every year. They include twelve-hour rallies, twenty-four hour rallies, and multi-day rallies. Their organizers develop some of these to be fun, some entertaining, and some to be a challenge. However, no other rally covers the time, complexity, and distance of the IBR, and no area of the world has the wide-open spaces and the road infrastructure to present the challenges to the riders that North America does.

2 How Did I Get To This Strange Place?

My name is Joel Rappoport and I'm the Safety and Health Manager of a packaging company in Winston-Salem, North Carolina. I'm also the Fire Chief of my company's industrial fire brigade and have been a volunteer fireman and emergency medical technician for three decades in Vienna, North Carolina.

I consider myself to be an ordinary kind of guy with one exception: I am addicted to long-distance motorcycle riding. Simply put, long-distance riding means regularly riding lots of miles, but the rub is defining "lots of miles". Many of the riders I know outside of the Iron Butt Association consider a two-hundred mile day as a long ride and a six-hundred mile day as a major undertaking.

On the other hand, most long-distance riders typically think little about riding over a thousand miles a day, day after day. It's just something we do, and riding across five states for lunch and returning home the same day is a fairly normal experience.

Long-distance riding involves being able to stay in the saddle for eighteen or more hours a day. It entails quick fuel stops, eating meals while traveling, and being comfortable enough in the saddle that stopping to stretch is unnecessary. It incorporates the love of riding, adventure, traveling, and finding new places to visit. It's exhilarating, exhausting, satisfying, and just plain fun.

That's where the addiction part comes into play. Whenever I'm on a long ride the everyday tension and frustrations drain away as the miles build up. The only reason that I won't ride my motorcycle on a given day is if there is ice or heavy snow on the roads, because all I can do on ice is fall down. In my hometown of Winston-Salem, North Carolina, that means the riding season is fifty weeks a year. During those two weeks I'm forced off of the motorcycle by the weather I go into withdrawal and get jittery and irritable, as over the course of forty years, riding has become an integral part of my method of coping with stress.

Endurance riding enables my rationale that going to the beach for lunch, a six-hundred mile round trip, is a short hop. Or that meeting a fellow rider two states away just to swap riding tales for a few minutes is a good way to spend a morning. After carrying on with this sort of riding for a few years, it became second nature and I stopped considering distance as a limiting factor when planning a ride.

Long-distance riding requires a sort of twisted mindset to accept the challenge of unfamiliar routes through strange lands with uncontrollable weather and unknown circumstances in order to greet the rewards of the adventure.

I wasn't always like this. I grew up in a fairly conservative setting in Trenton, New Jersey, in a family that did not tolerate the idea of "adventure". My range to play as a child was restricted to the block our house sat on. Vacations were always to the same places each year and we followed the same tried-and-true paths to get to them. Anything out of the ordinary was feared and to be avoided at all costs. It was a pretty dull existence.

The outlook for my future was kind of like an arranged marriage. I had always been told that I would be a lawyer. My family had plans that I would be a lawyer. My father was a lawyer and a Judge and he had a sign painted for his law office that included my name for when I eventually would join the practice. My father immensely enjoyed practicing law; it was his "thing" as he was happiest at the office and practiced until he died at seventy-nine. I would dare to say that practicing law was his adventure. But it wasn't mine.

By the time I went to college I was absolutely convinced I did not want to be a lawyer. I was a hands-on kid. I was tearing apart machines and devices from as early as I can remember just to see how they worked and most of the time I was successful in reassembling them. I played with electrical, electronic, and mechanical devices. In school I enjoyed metal shop, wood shop, and print shop. I loved to build things from wood or metal and to get my hands dirty. This last was frowned upon by my family and barely tolerated by my parents.

In 1971 I went "over the fence" and escaped. I moved to Winston-Salem to attend Wake Forest University which, by the way, had an excellent law school. More importantly, it was also the farthest college from Trenton that accepted me for enrollment. Distance, in this case five-hundred miles, was a good thing as I tried to shed the ball and chain of my dull past and uninspiring future. After the second year at Wake Forest I dropped out and went to work for a radio station as a disc-jockey. My parents said I was rebelling and I agreed.

Over the next year a lot of folks told me I was foolish for not finishing college. I listened to them and went back for another year and a half, but a liberal arts education was not what I was looking for in life. I wanted to build things, paint things, connect things, weld things, work with my hands, travel, and challenge the dull side of life. Practicing law, desk-work, and the tie-and-jacket trades were not remotely close to my idea of the good-life. I dropped out again and spent the next thirteen years in radio as an announcer, engineer, and finally as a talk show host.

In 1972 I took my first motorcycle ride on a rented Honda 250. The ride only lasted two hours because at fifteen dollars an hour that's all I could afford. That first ride involved mostly right turns since I had never used a clutch and couldn't quite cope with working the foot-brake, hand-brake, clutch, foot-shifter, and throttle while balancing the bike and watching for traffic coming in both directions, all at the same time. At the end of the ride I was hooked and for the past forty years a motorcycle has been my main form of transportation. I always enjoy riding, even if only traveling to and from work each day, as there is something about being on a two wheeled vehicle, with not much more than an engine and a fuel tank under me, that makes traveling an exciting undertaking rather than just a way to move from place to place.

Throughout the seventies I would climb on the bike every spring or fall and spend a month or more moving around North America. I would visit friends, camp out, and just ride to places I thought might be interesting. Through these years my father was waiting for me to come to my senses and "settle down"; while my mother made a very vocal production of crocheting afghans for folks as a way of coping with her irritatingly loud worries about my motorcycling. Everyone in the family got some really nicely made afghans except me, but I was enjoying what I was doing. I think that my father knew that I was having fun and enjoying life, but he had to stand by the "party-line". When I visited Trenton he would come out and look the motorcycle over, ask questions about my gear, and occasionally I would catch him wistfully touching the handlebars.

Long-distance motorcycle riding is different from other sports in that being "in shape" for rallying doesn't entail being physically fit, trim, buff, svelte, muscular, or what most folks remotely imagine to be "athletic". I'm five foot, five inches short, tend to stay around the one hundred and ninety pound mark, but look larger. That's a nice way of saying I'm overweight. As a fireman I regularly pull my weight (pun intended) at fire and rescue incidents, but after each strenuous emergency I tell myself that I have to start exercising. I rarely do.

Long-distance riders look for any excuse to travel and this is the reasoning behind many of the rides that the IBA offers. For example, the *National Parks Tour* entails visiting at least fifty National Parks in at least twenty-five states in one year. The *Ultimate Coast-to-Coast* necessitates traveling from Key West, Florida, to Deadhorse, Alaska, in thirty days or less. These and a host of other sanctioned rides give the motorcyclist a destination as well as a mileage or time limit to target. In other words, an excuse for a great ride.

This type of riding does take some getting used to in terms of physical and mental capability. For the first thirty years or so that I rode a motorcycle I considered a five-hundred mile day to be an extreme achievement. I would ride that distance from North Carolina to visit family in New Jersey a few times a year. This trip would take thirteen hours each way with at least a one day layover to physically recover before the return trip. I would ride for an hour and then stop to eat, ride another hour and stop to rest. It was a herky-jerky way to tour but it was the only way I knew.

In 2001 I started to make this trip every other weekend in order to visit an ailing relative. This was also around the time that I first heard about the Iron Butt Association and found that there was a twisted group of motorcyclists who enjoyed long-distance riding as much as I did. I began to change the setup on my BMW motorcycle as well as my attitude toward traveling, and the trips north got easier and easier. I focused more on appreciating the act of riding and less on waiting for the miles to roll by. Each ride became an adventure rather than a task.

On a trip north in 2005 I had an epiphany of sorts as everything on that ride to New Jersey coalesced. I rode north with only one quick stop for fuel. I felt fresh and ready-to-rock when I got to Cherry Hill, and when it was time to leave that night I hopped on the BMW and returned home with another single quick fuel stop. The travel time was seven and a half hours each way and I wasn't tired when I got back home. Total time on the trip was just under twenty-four hours. From then on I sought out any excuse I could find to put miles behind myself and the R60.

3 She's Old But She's Good

In 1976 I owned a Honda 450 with 65,000 miles on it. I had journeyed across the country and back on the Honda the year before, but I wanted something with more power and better handling. A friend had let me ride his 750cc BMW a few times and I was truly impressed with the ride, the sound, and the look of the bike.

At idle the engine loped slowly and had a particularly pleasing sound similar to a turn of the century hit-and-miss engine. On the road the Boxer was exceptionally smooth. The exhaust-note when accelerating was powerful and particular to BMWs, and the feel while riding could best be described as unshakable. But even though I wanted to buy a BMW, they were premium motorcycles and I just couldn't afford the price.

Back in the '70s BMW had a reputation as the most dependable and rugged motorcycle in the world, as well as leading the pack in terms of technology. BMWs were completing treks across the Sahara and Gobi Deserts, blitzing the mountain passes in Europe, Asia, and the U.S., as well as crisscrossing every nation on earth. BMW motorcycles were regularly ridden for hundreds of thousands of miles with no problems. In fact BMW had a program through its dealerships to award special metal mileage plates to affix to the motorcycle when the owner achieved multiples of 100,000 miles.

That January I was working as a disc jockey at a radio station in Richmond, Virginia, and received a press kit for the annual Daytona Beach, Florida, Bike Week races and festivities. I couldn't attend so I gave the kit to the owner of the motorcycle shop where I bought my parts. A few days after Bike Week he asked me to come to the shop to meet a friend of his who had traveled to Daytona with him. It seems that the press kit not only contained passes to the races, but included access to the pits and parties. It also covered their hotel stay and they had a blast. His friend owned a BMW dealership and made me an offer I couldn't refuse on a brand new Monza Blue 1976 BMW R60/6.

I named the R60 Entropy. I understood entropy as a theory of physics that states that everything in the universe will eventually wear down. But, it will take a long time to happen. I expected the R60 to last a long time. I had no idea just how long that would turn out to be. The R60 is the only motorcycle that I would own for the next thirty-three years. It was my main form of transportation for all of those years, and in fact I didn't own a car until 1981.

The R60 is a 600cc motorcycle and is referred to as an Airhead because the cylinder heads stick out from the sides of the engine and are cooled by the airstream moving past the motorcycle. It is also called a Boxer because the pistons move in and out horizontally (like a boxer throwing a punch). BMW introduced the Boxer engine back in 1923 and those cylinders extending out from the sides of the engine have been their signature for almost a century.

To a lot of folks this engine design made the motorcycle look crude or ungainly. The Airheads lacked chrome and many of the attributes that most people looked toward as attractive in a motorcycle. However, having the cylinder heads sticking out into the airstream for cooling has worked very efficiently and the Airheads are as reliable as a rock. I consider the bike beautiful and she has never let me down.

I've ridden the Beemer in desert heat, through hurricanes and near tornadoes, on back roads and interstate highways. Rain, heat, wind, cold; it didn't matter. I loved to ride and any excuse was good enough to get me on the bike.

During the first five years that I owned the BMW I would take a month away from work each year to ride around North America. The Beemer carried all I needed to be able to comfortably camp out as I explored the continent. As a volunteer fireman and emergency medical technician for over thirty years, the bike was equipped with red emergency lights and carried all of my firefighting and rescue gear.

At the start of the 2009 IBR the R60 had 512,000 miles on the odometer, and while this may seem excessive to some folks, it was normal to me as this was my only bike. I'd taken care of it for all of those miles and it served me well through thick and thin. I didn't consider it "high" mileage and didn't have any concerns about it covering the distance of the rally and then some.

This is not an ordinary R60, but a bike that I have constantly modified over the years to be the most comfortable place on earth and to make safe long-distance riding as enjoyable as possible. Anything that might annoy me, such as having tired muscles from stretching in a seating position that is not quite right, would take away from the joy of the ride; therefore this R60 was adapted to fit me.

If you wander around any IBA gathering and look at the motorcycles you will see machines that push the envelope of modern technology. Most host at least one GPS. Almost all have state of the art headlights and auxiliary lighting. CB radio didn't die in the seventies; it is still widely used by truckers and is a common sight on long-distance cycles. Tied into the CB are cell phones, navigation aids, radar detectors, and music players. One rider in 2007 had a satellite phone and his laptop wired into his communications gear. Auxiliary fuel tanks are common, as are satellite tracking systems.

Safety, comfort, and navigation equipment that long-distance riders add to their motorcycles are referred to as farkles. Where that name came from no one knows for sure, but it is particular to the long-distance community. Adding farkles to a motorcycle has to be well thought out because no rider wants to decrease the reliability of their machine. A lot of IBA riders spend an inordinate amount of time and money to integrate their farkles so that they look as if they came with the motorcycle.

The average motorcycle rider sees this additional equipment as unnecessary. I've had riders look the R60 over and tell me that there is no good reason for one GPS, let alone two. Other common comments: extra fuel isn't safe because a rider needs to stop every hundred miles in order to stay sharp, and listening to music while riding is distracting.

The farkles help make long-distance endurance riding safer, and more enjoyable. For example, improving the lighting makes it possible to see road hazards long before a stock headlight would illuminate them. Brighter and flashing stoplights are added to more quickly alert following motorists. Daytime running lights make the motorcyclist more visible to oncoming traffic. The ability to drink water while riding helps to prevent dehydration. Being able to listen to music prevents boredom, and can stave off fatigue.

As to the navigating equipment, if a rider is going to be successful in the IBR or any other rally, they need to know where they are and where they are going at all times. A single GPS would work. However, electronics can fail, and having a backup GPS is good insurance.

In 2008 the IBA held a National Meet in Denver, Colorado. A few of us were designated as Farklemasters and tasked with presenting seminars on how to properly add equipment to our cycles. The general idea was to give advice on electrically wiring, plumbing, securing, and understanding farkles. For example, my seminar covered understanding electricity and proper wiring. We dealt with adding radios, cell phones, navigation gear, headlights, and electrically heated clothing so that there was no chance of causing a motorcycle to malfunction. If done correctly, the equipment would work as it should and be easy to troubleshoot if it broke.

The R60 was a naked bike when I bought it in 1976. It didn't have saddlebags or any other type of storage, and there was no wind or weather protection. Over the next thirty-three years I made it the perfect Iron Butt motorcycle.

First off, the BMW had to be comfortable to ride for twenty hours a day. The Rocky Mayer built seat is custom fitted to my weight, height, and riding style. The reach from foot-pegs to saddle to handlebars is perfectly adjusted and I end up sitting with just a small amount of forward lean. I once rode over 3,000 miles in forty-eight hours on this saddle in total comfort, and for the IBR I added a sheepskin pad for just a bit more cushioning.

For 2009 I mounted a Hannigan fairing. A fairing is the fiberglass body-work and windshield on the front of the motorcycle which protects me from the weather as well as streamlines the bike for better handling and gas mileage. The Hannigan is an old design dating back to the early seventies, but has a well-earned reputation for making the motorcycle more stable than stock, improving fuel mileage, and deflecting rain and wind away from the rider. I also liked the fact that the Hannigan harmonizes with the appearance of the classic R60.

I left home at 3:00 p.m. on a Friday in March to cover the one thousand miles to Hannigan Fairings in Paris, Arkansas. I arrived at 9:00 a.m. Saturday, right on time for my appointment with Jerry Heil. We worked on the R60 all day, and at 9:15 that night I shook Jerry's hand, and headed out on the one thousand mile trip home. It was all good training for the IBR.

Inasmuch as I ride around the clock, I needed to be able to see clearly at night far in advance of the motorcycle and the lighting had to extend widely on either side of the road to help pick out deer, elk, buffalo, moose, bear, and the like. I replaced the 1976-era headlight with a state-of-the-art high intensity discharge (HID) low beam and added two HID driving lights acting as high beams. The lighting setup was completed with a set of fog lights to help the low beam light up the road.

In order to power the lights, the original 280 watt charging system was replaced with a high-output Omega alternator from Motorrad Elektric. This 500 watt system would also power my heated riding jacket, the navigation equipment, radio, computer, cell phone, and other electrical equipment.

The stock 5.8 gallon gas tank would reliably yield a 250 mile range, which is fine for motoring around town, but not for long-distance riding. I added a five gallon auxiliary fuel cell on a custom built rack on the rear of the cycle which feeds by gravity to the main tank. This comfortably increased my riding range to 450 miles.

Carrying more fuel obviously means that I can ride farther than the stock setup, but it also means that I can stop for fuel when I want to rather than when I have to. In parts of the U.S. and Canada there is no fuel available 24 hours a day, and in other areas gas stations may be three or four hundred miles apart.

I installed aftermarket LED tail lights for the ability to be seen better by other vehicles and the R60 also hosts a map light, large top-loading saddlebags, and a trunk on the rear to carry all of the special equipment needed for the IBR. There is a hydration system consisting of a one gallon water jug with a long tube ending in a bite-valve at the handlebars so that I can drink while moving. I also installed a bowl near the handlebars where I could place snack bars to eat while riding.

The snack bowl is visible under the handlebar. The one gallon water jug sits just in front of the saddlebag.

Lastly, I added the navigation equipment that was necessary for the rally. There are two Garmin 478 Global Positioning Systems (GPS), a CB radio, and a cell phone that are all linked together and feed through a headset in my helmet. With this setup I can talk with other riders or truckers on the CB radio, make and receive calls on my cell phone, and hear the special voice from the GPS giving me turn-by-turn directions to my destinations.

For routing during the rally I carried a laptop computer that ran Microsoft Streets & Trips mapping program. The trunk that the laptop traveled in was padded and equipped with a charging cord to keep the battery up to snuff. To get help in the event of an emergency, and to let my family know where I was riding, I used a SPOT personal satellite tracking device. The SPOT tracker contains a GPS and a transmitter. It kept constant track of my position and sent my coordinates to a satellite every ten minutes. My track was then displayed on a map on the internet.

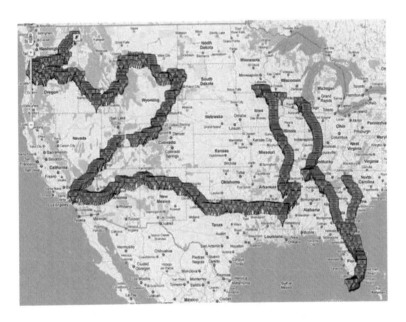

Here is the SPOT map of my 2009 Iron Butt Rally.
Markers show the ten-minute-coordinates and "OK" messages

My family kept track of my progress on a web page as I rode. Being on the road in distant, foreign, and unexpected places can lead to worries back home and since my wife, Susie, is my greatest cheerleader, I wanted to relieve her of as many concerns as I could. The SPOT has a feature where I can press a button to send an "I'm OK" email, as well as put a point on the map showing my location. I would do this every time I stopped at a bonus. I would also send this message whenever I stopped for sleep, and when I started riding again.

One other bit of information about the R60 is that for its first thirty-one years and 427,000 miles, no one but me had ever done any work on the bike. I carried out regular maintenance, tire changes, and rebuilds. Just before the 2007 rally I discovered a shop called Boxerworks in Watkinsville, Georgia. When the owner, Nathan Mende, heard that I was riding the R60 in the IBR he offered to help defray the costs of my ride with discounted parts and service as well as advice.

I traveled to Watkinsville four times to talk with Nathan before I finally decided to accept his offer of help. I wondered what Nathan thought of me because I would visit his shop, talk about BMWs and the IBR for hours at a time, and then disappear. I had never let anyone touch the R60 and I was skeptical that someone else would put the same care that I did into servicing the bike. I surely could use the expert help and I was flattered that Boxerworks-service was willing to work on the bike, but I was nervous as all get-out about whether he realized just how important this rally was to me.

I shouldn't have worried. Nathan was a BMW motorcycle fanatic who worked on all models from 1923 to the present. He knew the specifications of each model by heart, what parts interchanged amongst models, and what combinations worked or didn't work well together. Along with this he has a stash of new and used parts not found anywhere else and was more than enthusiastic about helping me succeed in the IBR on the R60. It helped a lot that Nathan also looks the part of a mechanic who works on old/exotic bikes. He can best be described as a grizzled, bearded, Gnome-like eccentric with a bit of mad-biker about him.

He and mechanic Dean Graham converted the original 1976 front drum-brake to a twin disc-brake system, rebuilt the engine and transmission, and offered enthusiastic best wishes. Boxerworks became my "local" bike shop. It was only a five hour ride to Watkinsville and going down to visit with the folks at the shop was a pretty nice way to spend a Saturday.

Now, the IBR is an amateur event and the organizers intend to keep it that way. They do recognize the large amount of money that riding in the rally entails and therefore allow limited aid for the riders, but there are explicit and unequivocal rules governing sponsorships. When you get down to brass tacks, no stickers or decals are allowed on the motorcycles. Only a handful of motorcyclists even know that the IBR exists, and coverage of the event in the media is just about non-existent. There is no real reason for a business or person to contribute to a rider's success except for the love of the sport.

The bike ran well during the 2007 IBR but I found that a 600 cc engine putting out forty horsepower was just not enough to keep me at the posted speed limits in the West for the nineteen hours of riding a day that I averaged through the rally. There was no reserve power for mountains and other similar conditions and I had to address this failing. To prepare for the 2009 IBR, Nathan and Dean convinced me to convert the 600 cc engine to 750 cc, which added ten horsepower. After looking back on the rally I realize that I made the right decision. The R60 (now R75?) performed flawlessly.

Dean carried out most of the mechanical work on the bike and Nathan provided expert advice as well as a discount on new parts and many used parts for free. The used parts included the cylinders, heads, pistons, and carburetors for the displacement conversion. While assembling the engine, they discovered that after a half a million miles the oil pump housing was slightly worn and suggested that I replace it. Trouble is that the housing is part of the engine block. Nathan thought that the current oil system would make it through the rally, but just in case he contributed a used engine block.

I already had over a quarter of a million miles on an Omega, high-output charging system which raised the alternator output from 280 watts to 450 watts. Rick Jones at Motorrad Elektric offered an upgraded Omega and spare parts for 2009. Looking at all of the extra electrical items on the bike for the rally, I was tickled for the help.

With all of these changes the BMW was extremely comfortable to ride, the engine was smooth and reliable, and I carried enough fuel to securely cover the miles. I also had the equipment to know where I was and where I wanted to be within a few inches and minutes, so it was now time to train for the ride.

At the end of this story I have included a list of everything I carried during the rally, and I carried a lot. All of it fit neatly on the bike and I kept a handy listing of where I had stashed each item. A rider who is going to make the investment in time and money to ride in the IBR must be prepared for every eventuality.

I carried spare parts for the BMW, extra navigation equipment, paper maps for every state, emergency medical equipment, a second camera, and backup cables for every electronic device.

The cockpit with two GPS units.

The rear case is for the laptop with the five gallon fuel cell just in front.

Note the top-loading saddlebags

4 I Join the Hopeless Class

When I tell folks that "I love to ride", it is more than just a catch-phrase, and long-distance riding is more than just a hobby. It's my way of life. Motorcycle riding is what I do to relax, to think, to just do something different. I smile a lot when riding and I really can't explain why. All I know is that after forty years I accept that riding is the best therapy for an otherwise wretched day, or the best way to cap off an outstanding one.

Let's talk briefly about "certifying" long rides. After a long-distance motorcycle ride some IBA members submit their fuel receipts and witness statements so that the Association can verify their ride. Most rides require two witnesses to the starting odometer reading and location of the trip, and two witnesses to the finish. The fuel receipts must be obtained at a maximum of every 350 miles, or at each corner of the route.

Other riders just put on the miles and don't really care one whit about the certificates. The paperwork simply means that the rider has been audited and has completed the ride. It can be considered a long-distance certificate of authenticity.

For most certified IBA rides the rider can pick their own start and finish locations and make up their own route. Whether I want a certification or not, keeping my paperwork for each ride in certification-order helps to get me in the habit of checking receipts for the information that the Iron Butt Rally organizers require as proof of the route traveled. This includes noting the date, mileage, time, and location of each stop.

Bun Burner 3000 GOLD
An Iron Butt Association Extreme Ride!

This is to Certify that in July of 2006, Joel Rappoport completed consecutive Iron Butt Association Bun Burner 1500 GOLD rides consisting of documented back-to-back 1,500-mile days. Mr. Rappoport's stunning ride on a 1976 BMW R60/6 covered 3,052 grueling miles starting in King, North Carolina continuing on to Rockford, Illinois, Fargo, North Dakota, Kansas City, Missouri and Nashville, Tennessee before ending in Claremont, North Carolina in less that 48 hours.

The Bun Burner 3000 GOLD, an extreme ride designed for an extreme rider, was conducted under very strict guidelines set forth by the Iron Butt Association. Only a handful of riders from around the world have managed to solve the equation of time, distance and endurance to complete the Bun Burner 3000 GOLD.

Michael J. Kneebone
President, The Iron Butt Association

My certificate for back-to-back 1,500 mile days.

It is pretty interesting to talk to motorcyclists about their long-distance riding and sort through the riders who truly ride the miles and those who suppose they can and therefore claim that they do. Everyone has their own way to enjoy motorcycling. But, to be truthful, I have lost count of the folks who have told me that they actually only rode a few hundred miles a day but figured that they could easily have gone on for a thousand or more.

My certificates serve as markers of my progress as a long-distance rider. I completed a *Saddlesore 1000* in 2003 with 1050 miles in the twenty-four hour period. In 2006 I certified what is called a *Bun Burner Gold* ride of more than 1,500 miles in one day. That same year I certified back-to-back *Bun Burner Golds* (also called a *Bun Burner 3000 Gold*) by riding over 3,000 miles in forty-eight hours. The Iron Butt Association has over 50,000 members, which means that over 50,000 riders have certified a *Saddlesore 1000*. To date less than 100 have completed a *Bun Burner Gold 3000*.

I love to ride and while some folks feel the need to stop frequently to "enjoy" the areas they pass through, I can do this while I keep on the move. On the *BBG 3000* I watched the sun rise in North Carolina as the ride started. The sun set on me that evening in Wisconsin and rose the next morning in South Dakota. Then it set the second evening in Illinois and rose again in North Carolina as I was approaching home and the end of the ride. In just two days I rode through dozens of major cities and small hamlets on Interstate highways and two-lane back roads. I rode through forests, plains, mountains, and lowlands. The weather was cold, hot, rainy, and sunny. Circumstances like these amaze me and are a large part of what keeps me riding.

In order to ride in the Iron Butt Rally the rider fills out an application which describes their riding experience, and any other information that they think may be of interest to the organizers. The applications are divided into groups for a random drawing. The groups include rally veterans, rally volunteers, rookies, unique motorcycles, and the Hopeless Class.

Every rally there a handful of motorcycles and riders that are extremely old, underpowered, ugly, or for some other reason deemed to be unlikely to finish. These bikes and riders make up the Hopeless Class. In a lot of cases these bikes and riders don't finish, but in other cases they do spectacularly well.

Ed Otto, who finished in tenth place on a touring motorcycle in 1993, entered the 1995 rally riding a 250cc Honda Helix scooter rated at about nineteen horsepower. Ed finished in twenty-second place, ahead of 17 modern, full-sized motorcycles! This gives weight to IBA President Mike Kneebone's feeling that it is the rider that determines how well one finishes in the IBR, not the motorcycle. The rider has to keep a clear head and be able to discern the best route from all of the available bonus locations. The rider has to cope with bad weather, bad food, bad health, bad roads, and the other trials and tribulations of an eleven-day rally. The rider has to be constantly sorting through options as the physical and mental stresses of the rally wear away at their soul.

Hoping to ride in the 2007 Iron Butt Rally, I emailed my application in May of 2006. I figured that this would be a long-shot. I had never ridden in a twenty-four hour rally, let alone a rally extending through eleven days. In fact, I had ridden in only one rally to that time, the Mini-Mason. This was a ten hour rally held in Virginia the previous Fall.

I checked my email ten or twelve times a day from the day I entered until June sixth, 2006, when I received the following from Rally Master Lisa Landry:

I know you have been waiting with baited breath for a letter from me – either the coveted YES letter or the dreaded Sorry letter. Well, this one is a little of both – the Good News/Bad News letter.

First the bad news – your name was not drawn in the main field draw for the 2007 IBR. I'm truly so sorry.

Now the good news: we entered your name in a second drawing for the Hopeless Class and you were successful in that smaller field! This may or may not be your first choice, but it does afford you a coveted starting position in the 2007 Iron Butt Rally.

If you are willing to ride the motorcycle you listed on your entry, please drop me a note.

Was I willing? I clicked on "reply" and sent an "affirmative" just as quickly as my fingers could move. I had expected all along that since I was going to ride a thirty-one year old motorcycle with close to a half million miles on it and only forty horsepower, the rally organizers would put me solidly in the "Hopeless Class". I was thrilled beyond belief that the R60 and I were going to be a part of the IBR.

Over the next year and a half all of the riders received an update from Lisa every few months. These included the latest rules, checkpoint information, guidance on insurance for the rider and motorcycle, and occasionally a veiled hint of the challenges ahead. I would drop whatever I was doing when one of these missives arrived via email. I wanted to make certain that I did not screw up any of the formalities. As the rally date got closer I reviewed all of the information to try and get my head ready for what long-distance riders refer to as The Big Dance.

Even though I rode in the 2007 rally, I was not an official finisher but a DNF (did-not-finish). Thirty three percent of the riders failed to finish the rally; it was a nasty shock. After years of preparation I had failed to gather the minimum number of bonus points needed to be considered a finisher. I was not as well prepared as I thought I was for the rigors of an eleven day, eleven thousand mile rally. My ability to digest the hundreds of bonus locations in the rally packet and to create a successful route was below par, as I concentrated too much on miles traveled and not enough on the points I needed to finish.

The 2007 rally was run with two legs. The first started in St. Louis, Missouri, and ended at the same location 5 days later. Bonus locations were spread throughout the Eastern United States and Canada.

Immediately after the bonus packets were handed out for both the first and second legs, the organizers offered counseling for the rookies. Mike Kneebone, one of the foremost long-distance riders in the world, was willing to meet with the first-time riders to help them sort through the bonus listings. I decided that I didn't need the help and went straight to my room to plan my leg. I don't know what I was thinking, passing up the offer of advice. It was the wrong thing to do.

I rode to Perce Rock in the Gulf of Saint Lawrence in northern Ontario, Canada. I was able to walk across the ocean bottom at low tide to get a bonus photo, and then ride back to St. Louis in four and a half days, while picking up other bonuses on the way north and back. I was in fifty-fifth place at the end of the leg, having covered a bit over 4,500 miles on the R60, and I was proud of the accomplishment.

On the second, and final, leg which lasted for six days, I made errors in judgment that cost me the finish. I again passed on the offer of guidance from Mike Kneebone. I don't think that any of the rookie riders took him up on the offer. Looking back, that was a massive mistake on my part.

The bonuses were scattered throughout the western United States and Canada. I decided to head for bonuses in Canada and Hyder, Alaska, instead of following what I now know was a better route through the western states.

I failed to stay hydrated in the western heat and on the second day of the leg I was melting down at a rest area along the Lewis and Clark trail. I couldn't sleep, I was physically uncomfortable, mentally depressed, and had realized that my route sucked. I felt drained and couldn't get myself together to continue riding. I called Susie to tell her that I was dropping out of the rally and she correctly figured out that I was dehydrated. She ordered me to get to a motel for some sleep, not set the alarm, and to start drinking large amounts of grape juice and water.

I also called the Rally Master, Lisa Landry, to tell her that I was not going to continue. Lisa told me that she too had come apart on day nine of her IBR and that I had to pull myself together and get moving toward the bonuses in California.

I checked into a hotel in a nearby town and followed Susie's advice. Three hours of sleep later I was feeling much better and ready to ride, but I was also looking over the bonuses that were available and realized that the forty horsepower, 1976 R60 was not going to be able to get me where I needed to be in order to get enough points to be an official finisher.

Knowing beyond a shadow of a doubt that I would not succeed was a bummer but I plotted a route that covered close to four thousand miles for the remaining three and a half days of the rally. I ended up just short of the number of points needed to officially finish. That is the nature of the IBR. Either you finish the rally or you don't. There is no gray area.

I ended the 2007 rally feeling beaten, downhearted, and depressed. To say that I was disappointed with my performance would be an incredible understatement. I was devastated that I had spent years in preparation and I had fallen short of my goal. Folks at home were congratulating me on riding in the IBR and I was explaining that I had not "finished" officially. To them it was a monumental motorcycle ride. To me it was abject failure.

Long-distance motorcycle riding is my sport. It is where I hang my hat in terms of my personal success as a rider and I ended the 2007 rally in tears as I pulled into the finish checkpoint. I had entered the World Championship event with high hopes and found that I wasn't anywhere near as prepared for the rally as I had thought.

For the 2009 IBR I submitted my application in early 2008. On April fourteenth of that year an email from Lisa simply said my application had been drawn for entry. I had been clear in the application that I was still riding the 1976 R60/6, and expected to be drawn for the hopeless class. Instead, the organizers had entered me in, and drawn me for the main field. This meant that I was not required to ride the R60, but could ride any motorcycle I wanted.

I had a conversation with Lisa a month or so later and she mentioned that I had not been drawn specifically for the Hopeless Class this time. I could ride the R60 or I could ride a modern motorcycle. I told her that the BMW was the only cycle that I owned, and I felt that I had to ride it this time around. She spent a fair amount of time trying to convince me that a modern bike would be a better choice. Lisa emphasized it would handle better, brake better, accelerate better, be more comfortable, and let me spend more time concentrating on routing and the rally rather than the mount. I admitted that all of her points were valid, but I was hardheaded about being on the R60. She gave it her best shot.

There were far more riders wanting to take part than the 100 starting spots offered in 2009. For many of the riders who entered, this would be their second or third attempt to be drawn from the qualified entries received. The organizers drew 100 starting positions and the field was set.

Riders who were offered a starting position paid the rally entry fee, were expected to digest the substantial rulebook, and started preparing their motorcycle and themselves for the ride of their lives.

Among the one hundred and one riders who would start the rally there were ten women, five were riding by themselves, and five were riding as a couple with a spouse or friend. Imagine, riding two-up on a motorcycle for eleven days. There were nine Canadians, two Australians, and riders from the UK, Germany, and Ireland.

Getting ready for the 2009 IBR which would be in August, I rode at least one *Saddlesore 1,000* every weekend starting in April of that year. In May I rode two *Saddlesore 2,000*s which involved covering 2,000 miles in forty-eight hours. I also completed an in-state *Saddlesore 1,000*. I covered a bit over one thousand miles in less than twenty-four hours within the State of North Carolina.

This sort of riding obviously entails good time-management skills for the most efficient use of a rider's time. That means that the rider must adjust to fewer hours of sleep than might otherwise be considered normal, as well as maximizing those hours set aside for rest. This brings us to the Iron Butt Motel. The Iron Butt Motel is what long-distance riders refer to when we stop for sleep at places other than motels or hotels. I've gotten used to sleeping in rest areas, parking lots, parks, and along the side of the road.

There is no wasted time for "check in" or "check out" at the Iron Butt Motel and there is always a vacancy. Granted, the Iron Butt Motel lacks all of the niceties of other roadside accommodations, but it is free and has locations everywhere. I spent most of the 2007 IBR stopping for rest at the Iron Butt Motel, but I decided that for 2009 I would try to stay in a real hotel or motel each night in order to be more comfortable and see if I could get a better quality of rest.

While we are talking about resting, it's worth mentioning that stimulants such as caffeine are discouraged within the IBA. The various five-hour energy boosters and similar supplements have been shown to be detrimental to continuous long-distance riding. The rider may get a temporary boost from the supplement, but then there is inevitably a drastic dip in energy. I stopped drinking coffee and most caffeinated beverages like soda two months before the rally. The result was that if I needed a boost of energy I could do it with a single glass of Dr. Pepper. I relied on a diet using carbohydrates and protein to keep my energy level balanced. Training for ten years to stay in the saddle for twelve to eighteen hours a day helped as well.

I look at each and every ride as an adventure, although some have more thrills than others. I set off on one Friday night in May for a 1,000 mile loop through Virginia, West Virginia, Tennessee, Alabama, Georgia, and South Carolina. Three hours into the ride, on Interstate 81 in Virginia, I ran from clear skies into heavy rain in a matter of yards. I noticed on the NEXRAD weather radar on my GPS that the weather-cell I had entered was changing from a yellow to red to an angry ocher color about the same time that the GPS announced I was entering an area with a Tornado Warning.

The rain started coming down in a solid mass and I slowed to fifty miles per hour, but as it was 11:45 at night there was fairly light traffic. Then it started to hail accompanied by a constant strong crosswind which was pushing the hail horizontally. Within a few minutes the hail was so deep on the Interstate that it covered the lane markers and the world looked like a snow-scape. I pulled to the side of the highway two times but realized that I was going to have to sit there for another forty minutes or so till the storm moved on, and the hail was starting to sting through my riding suit. There was no shelter or exit from the Interstate close by and the radar showed that I could be out of the storm in just a few miles if I continued south, so onward I rode.

As I was midway through the storm I saw a tractor trailer about two hundred yards ahead of me suddenly move to the median. It didn't drive there. It was sort of deposited there, as one second it was in the right lane and the next second it was in the median. I stopped in the middle of the Interstate and then asked the driver on the CB radio if he was okay and his reply was that he was "plumb stuck" and I should get moving to get clear of the storm.

I ended up following another truck in its left wheel track which squished a lot of the hail and ice-mash out of the way. Within a mile the hail stopped, another mile and the rain slacked off, three more and I was on dry pavement looking at the nearly full moon. When I stopped at the next rest area to open the vents on my riding gear (it was seventy-two degrees) I found that the small dog-dish I have on my fairing to hold snacks was full of melting hail. Through all of this the R60 was solidly planted and never missed a lick.

That June I found that I had time for an extended trip, so I completed a ride called a *100CCC,* which is one hundred hours coast-to-coast-to-coast. The rider is allowed fifty hours to cross the country and then fifty hours to cross back. The *100CCC* would let me check out the changes made to increase the horsepower on the R60 as well as the equipment that I would be using on the IBR. It involved riding 20 hours a day for four straight days, which would also let me know if my riding stamina was up for the rally.

On June ninth, a Sunday, I stood in the Atlantic Ocean off of Wilmington, North Carolina, just before midnight. Touching the ocean was a symbolic act to start the trip. Forty-six hours later I stood in the Pacific Ocean off of San Diego, and forty-five hours later I was standing in the Atlantic Ocean at Jacksonville Beach, Florida.

I had stopped at motels for four hours of sleep in Texas, on the way out and back. In San Diego I had been invited to spend my four hours of rest-time at the home of two IBA members. They signed my witness form, took the pictures of me standing in the Pacific, and gave me a comfortable place to sleep at the midpoint of the ride.

When I got to Jacksonville Beach I was still feeling alert and had to decide whether to find a motel and get some sleep in Florida before turning toward North Carolina and home, or to just head north. I decided that since I was only seven and a half hours from home I would head straight back to North Carolina. I was in my kitchen recounting the ride to my wife Susie at 9:00 a.m. Friday.

The only drama on this ride was at the very end. To document that I had arrived in Jacksonville Beach within the time limit, I had to get a computer generated receipt from a gas station. I filled up the bike with gas, but while the printer made a whirring noise, no receipt came out. The printer was out of paper.

I went into the store and found that both clerks would be happy to sign my ending documentation that states that I was in Jacksonville Beach at 11:57 p.m., but neither knew how to print a duplicate receipt. I got the paperwork signed and put away but without the receipt I couldn't prove my time to the IBA. I ended up taking a photo of the gas pump showing the gallons sold and had the time displayed on my GPS in the foreground.

I knew that this wouldn't work for an official time stamp and I was just about to head across the street to another open gas station. I could squeeze a few cents of gas into my tanks and get a receipt. As I was about to roll, one of the attendants ran out of the store hollering at me. They had figured out how to get a duplicate receipt and my ride was officially over.

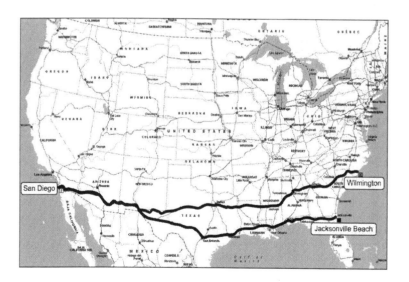

The BMW had made the trip without mishap. Even though the R60 was now a 750 cc motorcycle, I still was riding at near-full throttle for the four day ride. I had to add a quart of oil every 1,200 miles, but that's to be expected on an Airhead.

Standing in the Pacific Ocean at San Diego, California.

Notice the grin!

This is the kind of riding that I find exhilarating. This is my therapy and stress-relief for the twists and turns of life and this kind of riding keeps me sane (although some folks say it is obviously not working). The R60 finished the ride in good shape and all of my other equipment worked as planned, so I and the R60 were physically ready for the IBR.

Now let's deal with my mindset as the 2009 IBR began. After my first IBR I spent endless hours reviewing what I had done right and wrong, and when I was drawn for a spot in the 2009 IBR I was determined that I would not screw the ride up as I had done in 2007.

I now had a motorcycle that would cover the miles better than it had before. I had the equipment needed to get me safely through the rally. I knew that I could ride the miles and the hours and so I concentrated on routing.

I practiced by reading the bonus packets that were given out on previous rallies and getting the information sorted; therefore I could best judge which bonus locations were worth visiting and in what order to ride to them. I spent hours working with my computer's mapping software, entering bonus information, and adjusting routes. I re-read every piece of written information from previous rallies and pestered rally veterans for their strategies.

Tom Austin, one of the high mucky-mucks of the IBR, posted official internet updates for the 2007 rally. As the rally progressed he would write about which riders where choosing the "optimal" route and which were not. After the rally he dissected the routing options, the bonuses, and the timing, and his epilog describes a simple route that would have led to a finish with a moderate amount of miles ridden and a good night's sleep every night.

Tom is a great guy, but as I read his bit about the optimal finishing route I wanted to choke him. Tom is an engineer and has the natural ability to break a puzzle like the IBR down into its basic components and worry them around till he finds that optimal path. He also had a great deal of time to study the options prior to the start of the rally, as he is among the IBR staff who puts the rally together.

It was maddening to read his write-up of the finishing and winning routes describing how easily the puzzle could be solved. It was also educational because Tom was right. The insights into how to put a good route together are found throughout his story. I tried to come up with a template for dissecting the bonus packets based on Tom's suggestions.

Another rally veteran is Bill Thweatt. Bill has ridden in three IBRs and 2009 would be his fourth. Bill had moved from Texas to North Carolina a year before the rally and was only fifty miles south of Winston-Salem. We met a few times before the rally, and Bill hammered into my head that finishing the rally was not about miles but about points.

This seems like a fairly simple idea, but a rider faced with the fifty page list of bonuses while the clock is ticking and having to plan the next three or four or five or six days of riding with a good finish in mind can get twisted quickly. We talked about past rallies, strategies, and planning average miles per hour so that sorting bonuses can be an orderly process.

I settled on a forty-three mile per hour average for the rally. That is forty-three miles per hour averaged throughout each leg and including rest breaks, documenting bonuses, eating, and planning. In 2007 I had planned on a fifty mile per hour average speed. I had planned wrong.

Bill's advice helped a lot with my successful finish in 2009, and his willingness to help speaks to another remarkable part of the Iron Butt Association. Every member I've met has been more than willing to share their knowledge. Sure, there is competition amongst riders at the rallies but we are a small community; and if someone asks for advice on anything from outfitting their motorcycle to rally strategy, they can expect immediate help.

Here is the last major piece of my IBR. Almost all of the riders in the rally were on modern motorcycles and almost all of these were over 1000cc in size and their engines were typically rated at well over 100 horsepower. They sported the latest in suspensions, electrical systems, brakes, amenities, and handling ability.

In my case the suspension, brakes, handling, and mechanics of my bike were all based on the best technology that 1976 had to offer. I fully realized that this meant that I would be working harder to cover the same ground than riders on modern motorcycles. But, I was not riding the R60 because it was old, or underpowered, or a novelty bike, or to prove a point. I rode it because the BMW was the only motorcycle I owned.

The R60/6 was underpowered by most standards. Even with the extra ten horsepower from the engine rebuild, I would be lacking the acceleration and cruising speeds of the bikes that most of the field was riding. Then there was the wear-and-tear factor. There is no getting around the high-mileage on the bike and the chance of a component failure.

Lastly, there was me, the rider. I had failed to finish the 2007 IBR. The reasons don't matter; the result does. I would be starting in a psychological sump, wondering if I would be able to route correctly, ride correctly, and have the BMW perform well enough to finish the rally this time.

5 Can We Just Start This Thing?

-Two days to the start, Saturday, August 22 2009-

I arrived at 9:00 a.m. at the Marriott in Spartanburg, South Carolina, and began registration and tech inspection. The proceedings seemed endless, as there were over a hundred riders trying to pass through this pre-rally gauntlet at the same time. The only good point about this interminable process was that there was plenty of time to visit with friends, old and new.

The starting hotel in Spartanburg (photo by Steven Hobart)

The riders are from every walk of life - lawyers, teachers, plumbers, firemen, stone-masons, pilots, soldiers, farmers, nurses, homebodies, retired folk, and almost any other occupation you can think of. Every single one of us had the same goal: to finish the Iron Butt Rally. Some were aiming to win, some to be in the top ten, and some (myself included) just aspired to finish with a great big grin on our faces. We talked about our plans, our fears, old rally stories, and just about what was happening in our lives.

Most of these riders care very little about motorcycle brands or types of equipment used unless there is a distinct advantage that they can adapt to their own riding style. Riders would be on motorcycles produced by BMW, Honda, Kawasaki, Suzuki, Harley Davidson, Triumph, Yamaha, Moto Guzzi, and Victory.

During the morning, a fair number of riders and well-wishers stopped by to talk with me about the R60. They wanted to examine the modifications I'd made to the BMW so that it would carry me to success in the rally. Some folks reminisced about old motorcycles and their exploits in younger days.

We talked about the current "hopeless class", which consists of my R60, two 1976 Suzuki rotary-engine cycles, and a 1982 Honda GL1100. The rotaries are special because an RE5 tied for first place in the first IBR and the organizers wanted to commemorate the twenty-fifth anniversary rally by having two of them entered. One bike looked as if it was restored with care; the other bike was a bit on the rough side. Neither rider had any rally experience. I wished both riders good luck.

One other interesting event in the parking area was watching a particular entrant readying his motorcycle for the rally. This IBR veteran was from the United Kingdom and he had flown to the U.S., rented a motorcycle for eleven days, and was in the process of adding his farkles. These included a fuel cell, navigating instruments, and various other do-dads. After the rally he would return the cycle to a location on the other side of the country.

I would imagine that most rental companies figure that their riders will average a few hundred miles a day and expect to receive the bike back with at most a few thousand miles on it. Think of the surprise in finding eleven or twelve thousand miles instead.

Mike Kneebone is the President of the Iron Butt Association. Mike likes a level playing field and the IBA has set exacting rules for each certified ride. When the IBA staff certifies a ride it means that the rider actually rode the miles they claimed and fell within the time limits for the ride.

Mike followed a similar process in creating the modern Iron Butt Rally. The IBR was an exciting but poorly organized event in its infancy in 1984. Mike took over the rally in 1991 and turned it over to Lisa Landry in 2005. They have set goals and standards for the riders and staff that have led to the premier event that we have today. Everyone who rides in the rally knows what to expect ahead of time, what rules are in place, and how they are to be followed.

The rulebook covers almost anything that may happen during the rally. The rules start with defining safe and unsafe conduct, and the penalties that can be imposed on riders who practice the latter. The IBA and IBR continually preach that we must practice safe long-distance endurance riding. Nothing else will be tolerated and any rider who engages in unsafe riding faces disqualification.

The rules outline the organizer's definition of good-sportsmanship and the penalties for not adhering to their interpretation. They deal with bonus documentation, rider assistance, equipment that is allowed or not allowed on a motorcycle, and even the minimum size engine that will be permitted to enter.

There are pages of detail on allowable fuel capacity. No more than 11.5 gallons can be carried on the motorcycle, and any fuel not in the stock fuel tank must be in an approved fuel cell that is safely installed. During tech inspection the volunteers will check for proper mounting, safe plumbing, safe venting, and grounding of the tank to the frame of the motorcycle.

Another part of the rules deals with penalties for missing checkpoints or losing documentation of bonuses or fuel receipts. They also explain how a rider must document a bonus, what to do if it is impossible to follow the instructions in the bonus packet, and the rules for digital photographs of bonuses.

The IBR requires that each rider have a high amount of motorcycle insurance coverage and that each rider carry medical evacuation insurance that will cover getting an injured rider from the scene of initial medical care to a specialized facility, as well as moving a rider from a distant medical facility to one closer to their home. The last part of this section of the rules offers suggestions to the riders about personal medical coverage and road-service coverage for their motorcycles.

Finally, there are sections that deal with suggested equipment to carry on the motorcycle, what is acceptable rider support, how to deal with sponsorships, and a myriad of small items.

Riding-herd on everything that goes on is Lisa Landry. Lisa is an IBR veteran and the Rally Master. This is her rally. She has ridden to almost every bonus location to confirm that the location matches the bonus listing and that riders can comply with the requirements to score the bonus. Lisa keeps the volunteers and the IBA staff organized and on track and does the same for the riders. She arranges the banquets, the badges, the bonus packs, the actual bonuses, and several hundred other parts of the rally that no one suspects exists.

Lisa Landry is the Law with a capital L. If a rider thinks a bonus is scored incorrectly Lisa will make the ruling. Have a problem with the staff and Lisa will set everyone straight. Don't understand a bonus or a rule and Lisa will explain it. She is also one of the most gracious folks I've ever met.

Registration for the IBR involves three areas: documentation, education, and technical inspection. All of this is carried out by the volunteer staff. These are IBR veterans, their family members, and other riders who dedicate an immense amount of their time to the Herculean task of making the rally a success. They work throughout the months leading up to the rally by riding to each and every bonus location, confirming that the mass of documentation needed is ready, planning logistics, and trying to cover every contingency that may arise when this large an undertaking is launched. Without the volunteers there would be no IBR.

The first area of registration required that each rider acknowledge, while being videotaped, that we understood each and every rule of the rally. We signed legal releases stating that we were adults and realized that motorcycle riding can be dangerous. We had our cameras checked, and our digital storage cards that were used to record the bonuses certified, and finally we were videotaped for a rider introduction that would be used in *Hard Miles 2*, a movie of this event.

Then we moved on to tech inspection which was run by Dale Wilson, otherwise known as Warchild. Dale finished fifth in the 1997 Rally and he brooks no nonsense during these proceedings. Between his military bearing and his shaven head, most riders know to do exactly what he asks when he asks it. I mentioned a while back that less than one hundred riders have ever completed back-to-back 1,500 mile days and only a handful have done three 1,500 mile days in a row. Dale once rode seven consecutive *Bun Burner Golds.*

Helping Dale with tech inspection were Bob Broeking, Greg Roberts, Lisa and Tobie Stevens, Jim Culp, and John Harrison. During inspection the staff made sure that everyone's driver's license, insurance, and registration paperwork were in order. There was a general safety inspection of the motorcycle and then they turned us loose on an odometer check that took about forty minutes. This involved riding a fourteen mile odometer check route and comparing the mileage displayed on our odometers to the known course-length. The odometer check allows the organizers to have exact mileage figures at the end of the rally.

A simple odometer check would be to ride in a circle around the hotel, but nothing in this rally is simple. The riders were expected to follow the directions, to the letter. If they missed a turn they would have to return to the hotel and start all over again. Here are the directions that each rider was given.

* * * * * * *

1. Place the front axle of the bike over the Start Line and zero out your trip odometer.
2. Exit the Tech Inspection lot and turn RIGHT onto N. Church Street.
3. At 0.7 miles you come to a large 'Y' intersection. Do not bear right, stay straight onto Asheville Hwy.
4. At 3 miles, you come across a large traffic circle. TAKE BUSINESS 85 SOUTH TOWARDS GREENVILLE (from where you entered the traffic circle, this exit is approx. 270-degrees around the traffic circle).
5. Travel south on this highway (it will turn into I-85 at some point) and take exit 68 (Greer Street). This is a long 2-lane "frontage" road that parallels the highway. Stay in the left lane, ending with a stop sign.
6. Turn LEFT at this stop sign, pass over the highway, then RIGHT onto the on ramp to head back north on I-85 towards Spartanburg.
7. Take the first exit you come to (Exit 69) which is Business 85 toward Spartanburg.
8. Stay on this road to Exit 4. Take Exit 4 (which will display as exit 4a) toward Asheville Hwy and Hwys 176 and 56.
9. This Exit 4 off ramp places you back into the traffic circle. Depart the circle by taking 56 East towards Spartanburg.
10. Stay on this 56 East which eventually turns into N. Church Street at the 'Y' intersection mentioned above. Continue on N. Church Street toward the Marriott.
11. Turn LEFT at the intersection of N Church Street and Daniel Morgan Avenue.
12. Make an immediate RIGHT into the Tech Inspection parking lot and place front axle over the Start Line.
* * * * * * *

It may not seem to be complicated to you, but to many of the riders it was as convoluted as a process can be, especially when they were mentally gearing up for the rally and already felt like rats in a maze.

On the way back to the hotel from the odometer check I had an encounter that set the tone that this was going to be an interesting rally. As I stopped at a red traffic light a few blocks from the hotel, Bob Higdon pulled up next to me. Bob is this year's route-master and he came up with all of the bonuses and the theme for the rally. Bob is a longtime part of the IBA, an IBR veteran, and one hell of a fierce endurance rider.

He had recently completed a five-year, 150,000-mile ride to visit the county courthouse in every one of the 3,069 counties in the lower forty-eight states. Rides that have themes like this give riders destinations to visit and a distinct reason to ride. Bob has also ridden around the world. He is not one for half-measures.

Bob has written extensively about long-distance riding, BMWs, and motorcycling in general. His style of writing might best be described as a down-to-earth Hunter S. Thompson with a bit of wry humor, and as the official IBR scribe, he posted the rally updates on the IBA website for the past five rallies. He also sports the same foreboding visage as Warchild. His quasi-scowl and bald head go a long way toward making folks think twice about approaching him, but he is good-folk and I think highly of Bob. In terms of all things related to long-distance riding he's The Man.

So, we were stopped at the traffic light and I was excited that I was finally getting close to the rally start and here was one of the Big-Kahunas right next to me. What words of wisdom and encouragement would Bob utter? Maybe he would offer a clue as to the rally theme or what to expect? I looked to the right, nodded and said "Good to see you Bob."

He grinned warmly and replied "I see you're riding that same old piece of shit again this year." I chuckled at this and didn't take it as disparaging toward me or the R60. After all, we were in the Hopeless Class and I was used to the second-looks that come when I tell folks that the Boxer and I would be in our second IBR this year. I also appreciated that Bob was a lifelong BMW rider and was inordinately familiar with the strengths of the Airhead and the hardheadedness involved in riding one in the IBR.

The light turned green so we moved on to the next red signal and stopped where I bubbled out "Yeah and I can't wait to get started." Still grinning, he slowly shook his head and noted "You didn't learn anything at all last time did you?" The light turned green and we rode to a momentary stop at the last red light before the hotel. As the light turned green I parted with "See you tonight." Bob smiled and we both rode on.

Months before the rally the riders were told that Bob Higdon would be the Route Master and he would be laying out the bonuses. Bob had recently completed his county courthouse ride and many riders thought that courthouses would be the theme of this year's rally.

On the other hand some of us had noted that Spartanburg, St. Charles, Santa Ana, and Spokane all were checkpoints and all started with the letter "S". This led to speculation that the winning route would be in the shape of an S. All of this was sheer speculation because no one but a select few IBR staff actually knew what bonuses would be offered.

When we saw the artwork for the rally shirts on Saturday we realized that the theme had nothing to do with courthouses or the letter S. It was to visit the-scene-of-the-crime. Some scenes were grisly and some were funny but everything related to a crime of some sort.

There was a mandatory media seminar late that afternoon where the organizers dropped a bombshell. They had read on the internet that several riders intended to blog or tweet throughout the rally about where they were, what they were doing, and where they were heading. This presented the staff with some problems.

Obviously, a blogging rider is not fully concentrating on the rally, riding, and safety. There was also a good chance that a blogging or tweeting rider would give out bonus information before the staff wanted it released to the general public. In a past Iron Butt Rally someone had hacked the IBR website and then announced the bonus locations as the leg was being ridden. This led to fans showing up at bonuses to cheer the riders on, and this resulted in confusion.

We were told that anyone who blogged or tweeted, other than to let their immediate family and friends know of their progress, would be disqualified.

We were also told that all SPOT and other tracking results would have to be password protected. It was alright for friends and family to know the password, and follow the rider. However, there would be no public tracking. This ruling would upset quite a few of the folks who had intended to follow the riders via their SPOT pages.

Saturday night was a social gathering where the riders all traded tales, worries, and stories of conquest or defeat and generally had a good time. It was the last night to relax before the serious business of the rally began. I spent time talking with Bill Thweatt and Tom Loftus at dinner. Tom finished 8th in the 1997 IBR and has ridden in six of these events. A lot of our discussion centered on why we do what we do.

Why commit to riding in the most demanding motorcycle challenge in the world? Why spend the substantial amount of money that the IBR requires as an entry fee as well as the funds needed to ready our motorcycles for the rally? There is also a fair financial investment in the ride itself in terms of fuel, tires, oil, lodging, tolls, etc.

Then there is the investment of time. Time spent riding in advance of the IBR to make sure that the motorcycle and rider are ready for the challenge and time spent riding in the rally. The rally lasts eleven days, registration takes two days, and getting to and from the rally takes even more time. I was lucky that the start was only two hours from my home. However, the finish would be in Spokane, Washington, and it would take me two days to cover the 2,655 miles to get back home.

After two hours of talking we came to the understanding that we do this because we love it. We love having the stories to tell about surreal riding, of overcoming miserable weather conditions, motorcycle failures, and a host of other concerns. Not every story ends in happiness or success but they all end with us learning a bit more about ourselves.

I also realized that it wasn't just the stories, but the pattern behind the stories. We get a kick out of the concept that we will be visiting places that we have never heard of. For that matter, some of the bonus locations are places that we would usually avoid. We will ride over roads that, in some cases, don't appear on a map. Some of these roads are well paved, and beautifully designed. These are a true pleasure to follow. Others are goat trails that test the ability of the motorcycle, and rider, to stay in one piece. We constantly reassess time, distance, and miles to finely hone our route, and have to be ready to ride through any weather, road and traffic condition, and personal affliction.

We may not agree on motorcycle brands, or politics, or other day-to-day concerns, but we all embrace the idea that long-distance riding is fun. After dinner I headed to bed for the last full night's sleep for the next few weeks.

-One day to the start, Sunday, August 23 2009-

Sunday was mostly free time for me, but I did attend two mandatory seminars before the evening banquet. One seminar concerned fatigue and was given by Don Arthur, a long-distance rider who just retired as Surgeon General of the Navy. Our armed forces have spent a lot of time and money examining fatigue management and Don was able to pass on some of the findings that could help us to ride safely. The other seminar, conducted by Bill Watt, was on the media and emphasized being very thoughtful and concise in any words that a rider might utter to a member of the fourth estate.

The organizers and staff repeatedly reinforced the notion that even though the IBR is the World Championship of long-distance endurance riding, it is still only a secondary concern in our lives. The riders must never forget for a moment that our families must be our most important consideration. This was underscored time and again. We were to arrive safely at the finish-line; nothing else mattered.

To remind me of this I have photographs of my wife laminated to the dashboard of the R60. Susie is absolutely relentless in her support but I know that she worries a lot about what can happen when I disappear on a long ride. The SPOT tracking device helps a bit, my ability to call her on the cell phone while riding helps a bit, and my reassurance to her that I won't do anything stupid helps a bit.

Photos of my wife and Big Dog

The photos of Susie include our dog, who gave me food-for-thought as I rode. Big Dog was rescued from twelve years as a junkyard dog where he was kept on a short chain. He now runs free for the first time in his life and even though he is old and in failing health he enjoys every minute that he is experiencing new things, smells, sights, and places. Big Dog can't see well at all and is deaf but that hasn't stopped him from going wherever his nose leads him and having fun while doing it. There are a lot of similarities between Big Dog's new found freedom and my IBR ride.

There was a riders' meeting at 2:00 p.m. and as I was waiting for it to begin, Nathan and Dean from Boxerworks stopped by the hotel to wish me luck. Actually, they spent a good bit of time walking around the parked rally bikes, and looking them over. They made a few comments about all of the advanced technology on exhibit. Since the majority of the motorcycles they work on are classic bikes, they were astonished at what was parked out front. I was really glad to see them, and thanked them again for the work they had done on the BMW.

In the riders' meeting we were instructed to be at our motorcycles precisely at 8:30 a.m. Monday morning to have our riders' card stamped and odometer read.   A rider who missed the deadline would not be allowed to start until all the other riders had left at 10:00 a.m.

Tom Austin went into great detail about the rules we would be following. He also noted that the USB thumb drives we were being given, which contained the electronic waypoints of each bonus, were encoded to identify each rider. He made it clear that sharing the files with any other person would be grounds for disqualification.

Then it was finally time for dinner, which was more of a business meeting than a meal, and after we ate, the first leg rally packets were distributed and everyone got serious. The packets contained forty-five pages of bonuses. There was a description of each bonus, what the rider was required to do to document the bonus, and an explanation of why it was included in the rally.

Along with the bonus packet each rider was issued a rally identification card on a lanyard that we were instructed not to remove from around our neck for the entirety of the rally. The laminated card had emergency telephone numbers and contact information. The lanyard was imprinted to resemble the crime scene tape that police use and said *Crime Scene – Do Not Cross*.

Lisa Landry reviewed the bonus packet and went into detail concerning a few bonuses. One bonus that was worth an enormous amount of points was an example of an impossible bonus. The Saanich Peninsula Hospital in Saanich, British Columbia, was worth 12,683 points. But, with sixty hours available to ride on the first leg and 5,100 miles to cover, it would be impossible to score. A rider would have to average eighty-five miles per hour for the leg. Lisa was telling us not to reach too far in our routing.

There were several other bonuses that she brought to our attention. They were consistent with the theme of the scene-of-the-crime but she felt that these particular crimes were too heinous to include in the rally. Since they had already been printed in the packet, she had assigned them a large amount of negative points to discourage us from visiting them.

Almost every rider understood the situation and crossed these off of the bonus list. However, one rider mentioned later that he may just visit the bonuses in order to have fun with the organizers. His plan was to miss one required item that was needed to document the bonus on the rally packet so that he would not incur the negative points. In reality, he too had mentally eliminated the bonuses in question because there is no time to spare for humor, even twisted humor, in the Iron Butt Rally.

There were a few last minute clarifications about the rules and we were turned loose to plan our fates. We had until the start of the rally to plan our first leg. This was the only time we would be planning our ride while off of the clock. Planning for legs two and three would be done while the rally clock ticked away.

6 Leg One - Spartanburg to St. Charles

Throughout this story there are sections of text in *italic type*. These are portions of the rally instructions taken directly from the rally packet with the kind permission of the IBR. Each rider was given their packet at the start of each leg. It contained all of the bonus information and any other material that the rider might need for the leg.

The fuel log bonus was first thing that the rider saw when opening the rally packet.

* * * * * * * * * * *

A maximum of 1,000 points total is available for fuel purchase records. To obtain points for fuel purchase records, riders must submit a receipt for every fuel purchase with the following information on the receipt: 1) location (city/town and state/province), 2) date, 3) time, and 4) volume (gallons or liters) purchased. If any of the required information is not printed on a receipt, it must be hand written on the receipt.

* * * * * * * * * * *

The fuel log serves various purposes. At the scoring table it allows the scoring staff to ensure that the rider is not carrying more than the maximum amount of fuel allowed in the rules. It also allows them to calculate the fuel used versus the mileage claimed versus the time involved to make sure that the rider has actually traveled to the bonuses being claimed.

In past rallies some riders have attempted to claim bonuses by getting information or items needed to prove that they visited a location without actually having ridden to the bonus. This is considered cheating. A computer algorithm used by IBR staff will flag these "reinterpretations" of the rules. A loss of the bonus points being claimed or possible disqualification from the rally can follow swiftly.

We had been told the location of the starting point, two checkpoints, and the finish location several months before the rally started. With this information we could reserve rooms at the hotels and make arrangements for supplies to be cached for use during the rally. We would start in Spartanburg, South Carolina. The first checkpoint was in St. Charles, Illinois, outside of Chicago. The second checkpoint was Santa Ana, California, near Los Angeles. The finish was in Spokane, Washington.

I had a feeling of dread as I looked over the list of one hundred and twenty-five bonuses and got a feel for what the high and low values were. I enjoy riding my motorcycle for endless miles but have never been one to have fun with puzzles. In fact, I don't do puzzles, read puzzles, or enjoy any part of the concept. I can state with absolute finality that I don't like puzzles at all. Well, the IBR provides those endless miles but it is also the mother of all puzzles. Sigh.

In past rallies some bonuses have been worth as much as a million points, and trying to keep mental track of where a rider stands in terms of high point values can get hairy. I immediately noticed that for this rally the average point values were extremely low. Low values fell between one and one hundred points, medium values were one hundred to two hundred, high values were two hundred to one thousand points, and very high values were around two thousand points.

This made it much easier for me to grasp mentally, and after I got this sorted out I entered each bonus location into my Streets & Trips mapping program on my laptop and read the requirements for scoring the bonuses.

I saw two routes which would exceed the 9,000 points that we had just been told would be a guideline for finisher status on this leg. The next checkpoint was in St. Charles, Illinois. A rider could go east to Martha's Vineyard, Massachusetts, and on to the checkpoint in St. Charles, or south to Key West, Florida, and on to St. Charles. I smiled at this because I always enjoy watching the expression on folk's faces as I describe routing in the IBR. When I explain that the best way to get from Spartanburg, South Carolina, to St. Charles, Illinois, is via Key West, Florida, it just blows some folk's minds.

-Day One, Monday, August 24-

Murphy's Law states that if something can go wrong, it will, and as I was dressing prior to the start of the rally I came face-to-face with Murphy. I had spent years getting my riding gear and my motorcycle ready for this eleven day event. The riding suit, boots, and gloves had been selected with long-distance riding in mind and relentlessly tested for fit and reliability.

As I pulled on my two-year-old riding boots I noticed that the inside padding above the big toe on my left boot had come loose and was pressing uncomfortably on my toe. A motorcyclist shifts gear with the left big toe against a lever. You lift your toe against the lever to shift into higher gears and press down on the lever to shift to lower gears. The R60 has a five-speed transmission and shifting gears to match speed and riding conditions is a continual process. I couldn't reach my fingers or a knife into the area that was coming loose in the boot and was only minutes away from the start of the rally. There was nothing to do but get on the bike and ride. But this was going to be an annoyance throughout the rally and was the last thing that I needed to happen.

I then headed to the motorcycle impound area for the rider meeting where we got a few rule and bonus clarifications from the staff; then we all wandered around shedding nervous energy until the rally start at 10:00 a.m.

As we mounted our motorcycles for the start, I was parked next to Rick Miller, who is a rather large and friendly rider on a rather large, bright yellow, Honda Gold Wing, and we wished each other luck.   I then became even more impatient to start as Rick lit up a huge cigar and I realized that I was directly downwind and the smoke was making me queasy. At least this took my mind off of the wait.

Waiting for the start. (Photo by Rick Miller)

At five minutes before ten, the two 1976 Suzuki RE5s were let loose from the impound area to a round of applause from both onlookers and the other riders. They headed out through Spartanburg where the local police department was working at each intersection to help us get through the city.

Exactly at ten o'clock the rally started for the other ninety-nine riders.   Dale Wilson walked down the lines of waiting motorcycles, pointed to riders who then let out their clutches and headed to the first bonus. At 10:02 a.m. my rally started and I was headed for the Interstate and the BMW bonus which was only 20 miles away.

The start (Photo by Steve Hobart)

* * * * * * * * * * *

BMW Visitor's Center   *666 points*
Monday, August 24 10:30 a.m. to noon
Greer, South Carolina

Park in the visitors' lot nearest the coordinates and walk approximately 100 yards to the museum entrance. Once inside, take a photo of Ed Culberson's 1981 R80G/S, Amigo.
Category: *Failure to keep making one of the more reliable Iron Butt motorcycles ever built.*
In 1985-86 Amigo became the first vehicle to travel the length of the western hemisphere nearly from pole to pole. Ridden by Ed Culberson, a retired Army officer and chief MSF instructor, the motorcycle survived unimaginable hardships during the journey, including a 12-day trek through the Darien gap. That unfinished section of the Pan-American Highway, 67 miles of trackless jungle between Panama and Colombia, had never previously been traversed by anyone except on foot.
*   *   *   *   *   *   *   *   *   *   *

The IBR folk sometimes put a bonus with a large point value fairly close to the starting location, and they say that they do this so that the new riders can learn quickly what is needed to successfully score a bonus, and so that they would be able to shoot video of the riders for a movie called *Hard Miles Two.*

I really think that they do it for their own amusement; so they can watch the pandemonium of 101 riders trying to grab the same bonus at the same time.

The first bonus in 2007 was the scene of much hullabaloo at the Gateway Arch in Saint Louis, which was less than a half hour from the start. That bonus required parking in a parking deck, and hiking two hundred yards in 98 degree heat and 100% humidity to take a photo in the visitor's museum under the Gateway Arch.

It also required passing through a metal detector. I and other riders were told at the entrance to the museum (in the leg of the Arch) that we could not enter with our pocket knives, so we had to return to the parking lot to stow them away and then hike back to the Arch.

Meanwhile, almost all of the riders waited in a long line at the Arch's entrance closest to the parking lot. Several of us figured out that the entrance at the other leg of the Arch didn't have a line and were able to get in and out in just a few minutes.

There was humor in the BMW bonus. The rally theme this year is *the-scene-of-the-crime* and quite a few BMW riders in the past decade have been stopped hard in their tracks when the final-drive that connects the transmission to the rear wheel on their motorcycle failed with no warning. This failure seems to happen more often to long-distance riders than to folks who ride a few thousand miles a year.

Typically, a mere moment before a failure occurs the rider feels as if there is some looseness in the rear wheel and then they are sidelined by the failure of the main drive bearing as it disintegrates. A number of riders have had this happen two, three, or even four times, and some riders think that it is a crime that BMW doesn't make a reliable motorcycle any longer.

As a matter of fact, three of the top riders who have a very real chance to win this event have taken precautions against final-drive failures on their BMWs. Two of them are carrying a spare, thirty-five pound, $1,200 final-drive unit in their kit. This is the equivalent of a car driver carrying a spare rear axle and differential in the back seat just-in-case. The other rider has changed motorcycle brands from BMW to Honda. My R60 has an older design for its final drive and failures are nearly unheard of.

I saw the humor when we found out that the point value at the museum would be 666 points during the pre-rally banquet. This prompted a rider to raise his hand and ask if the organizers "really" meant to have "666" as the value. When told that it was not a typographical error the rider then shook his head in disbelief. Finally, I was amused that 96 motorcycles bearing 101 riders who were ready to ride relentlessly to the far ends of the earth were all pulling into the same parking lot less than 20 minutes after the start.

The bonus wasn't available until 10:30 and everyone had to wait until that time to score, while they were chomping at the bit to get moving on the rest of the first leg. Well, not every rider was waiting. As I entered the building two riders came out having taken their photos and headed toward their bikes. I hoped they realized their mistake and returned before they were told at the scoring table in St. Charles that the points were invalid.

The BMW museum was a small space and was crammed to the gills with riders. A fair number of them were trying to pre-place their rally flags on the motorcycle that we had to photograph and a BMW employee was repeatedly telling them that this was a museum and not to put anything on the exhibit. I'm sure we put on a great show for the IBR staff as everyone was trying to decide just when 10:30 had arrived. Cell phone clocks, camera clocks, the wall clock, dead-reckoning by the position of the planets, and no one time really agreed with any other.

When my camera clock said 10:30 I handed it to another rider who snapped a photo of me holding my rally flag and then I took his picture with his camera and then we're off.

As I left I heard someone say loudly that they were going to wait five "extra" minutes "just to make sure" that the time was right. I hope that someone eventually explained to them that there are no "extra" minutes in the Iron Butt Rally.

A quick word here about the bonus pictures. In previous rallies the riders documented a visit to a bonus with a Polaroid photograph. There just isn't time during a rally to take 35mm film photographs and get them developed before scoring. With a Polaroid instant photograph, the rider would know, while still at the bonus, if the photograph they just took was acceptable as documentation. Most riders would use a marker to note the time, mileage, and bonus name on the Polaroid itself.

Just prior to this rally Polaroid stopped making their film so the organizers announced that those riders who still had film available could use it, but digital photographs would be the new norm. They set a standard for the resolution, or sharpness, of the pictures at 480x640. This is the lowest quality photograph that most cameras can take, but is close to the sharpness of the old Polaroid photos used in earlier years. For this reason, the bonus photographs here may seem a bit grainy.

The IBR folks did not want to spend endless hours at the scoring table enlarging and playing with digital photographs in order to see if the object they wanted was actually in the picture. They specified low resolution so that the rider would get up close and personal with the bonus and move on.

My plan for the first leg was to get two Florida daylight-only bonuses, then the Key West bonus, and finally work my way north on the second day, getting most of the other bonuses available in Florida. I will then have one bonus in Georgia and one in Tennessee before heading to St. Charles, Illinois, for the checkpoint.

I figured that this would allow me to get to Key West at night and return before dawn so that I could avoid traffic. Though there were many other bonuses available, especially in the Chicago area, I wanted to get to the checkpoint for early scoring so I could check the engine on the R60 and then get a good night's sleep.

Planning involved not only the time-speed-distance equations that every rider had to deal with but the fact that I was aiming to make this rally enjoyable. Seeing new places, pushing myself and the R60 harder and farther than ever before while grinning all the way was my goal.

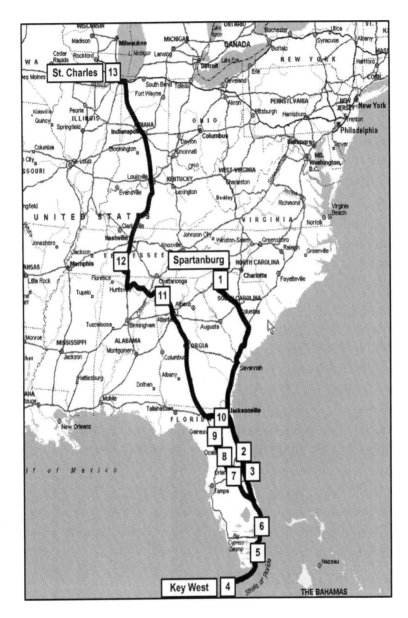

The first leg. Spartanburg to St. Charles.

There were sixty hours to ride on the first leg and my
route was roughly 2,715 miles and took forty-eight of those

hours. I planned on four hours of sleep sometime Tuesday morning after I returned to the mainland from Key West, and if I was ahead of plan I could add a bonus or two near the checkpoint.

The points-per-mile-ridden on the later legs of an IBR are always higher than during the first leg. Yet every rally there are riders who wear themselves out on the first leg and are never able to recover before the eleventh day. I didn't intend to be among them.

I left the BMW Visitor's center and headed to Harbor Oaks, Florida, for a 504 point bonus. Harbor Oaks was seven hours and 497 miles of Interstate riding from the BMW museum. It was available "anytime" and on the direct route to Key West. After years of preparation I could finally settle in and ride.

* * * * * * * * * * *

The Last Resort   *504 points*
Anytime
Harbor Oaks, Florida
Take a photo of the exterior of the bar.
Category: Serial murder.
Aileen Wuornos, America's most prolific female serial killer, was captured here on the evening of 1/9/1991. At the time of her arrest she and her girlfriend were living in Room 8 of the Fairview Motel a few hundred yards south of this bar. The room contained a three-dimensional replica of The Last Supper.
* * * * * * * * * * *

There were four other riders at the bar as I pulled up. I documented the bonus by taking a picture of the bar with my rally flag in view, and noted the time and mileage on my bonus scoring sheet. What was puzzling to me was that three riders were still at the bonus when I left. The way to succeed in the IBR is to keep moving. This is a lesson I learned in 2007. I realized on the second day of the rally that spending time talking with folks at the bonus location or with other riders was time wasted.

Here's my bonus routine. I stop so that the BMW is in front of the bonus and place my rally flag over the motorcycle or in front of the bonus itself. The flag is given to each rider at the banquet and is specially made for each IBR. It has the rider number, in my case number "three", and a unique design and color.

Since the flag has to be in virtually every picture, the IBR staff are assured that the rider visited the bonus location during the rally. Losing the flag means losing bonus points at the finish as well as having to have the rider's face in each bonus photo.

I then snap the picture, after which I re-read the bonus instructions to make sure I've done exactly what the organizers require, and return the camera and the flag to the inside pocket where they stay for the entire rally. The camera and flag are both clipped to the pocket with small carabineers.

Finally, I write the date, time, and mileage information on the rally sheet. If any of the information is missing or incorrect or if the picture is not correct the bonus points will be denied.

Stories abound of riders who have ridden thousands of miles for a bonus and then been denied the points because they forgot to include their rally flag, or photographed the wrong sign, or left off a bit of documentation.

In 2005 a rider traveled from the start in Denver, Colorado, to Key West, took a picture of the southernmost point in the continental US, returned to the checkpoint in Denver, and found that he had forgotten to include his flag in the photo. He had ridden over 4,500 miles in a bit under four days. He did not receive any points for the bonus.

This is the challenge of the Iron Butt Rally. A rider must be able to keep their wits about them, have excellent reading comprehension, and safely complete the rally with a high score.

The information that the rider records on the bonus sheet is used to verify that they actually visited the bonus location. At the scoring table and during audits carried out after scoring, the rally organizers will check the miles traveled against the time entered against the amount of fuel consumed according to the fuel log.

Throughout this story it may sound as if the IBR has taken control of how and when I acted, moved, and functioned. It had. But in other ways this control leads toward success in riding the rally. I have trained for years to keep certain items in certain pockets and check regularly to make sure that they are where they should be. This means that there is that small bit less to worry about. Worry leads to fatigue and fatigue is every rider's bane.

Titusville was just forty-two miles away and was the last bonus before Key West. The bonus was a pleasant park and I easily took my photo, filled out the log, and got ready for the ride to Key West. What was not pleasant were the pitch black clouds that had gathered overhead and to the south.

*   *   *   *   *   *   *   *   *   *   *

Veterans Memorial Park   *713 points*
Daylight hours only
Titusville, Florida
Take a photo of the Project Mercury memorial sculpture near the men's room at the far (eastern) end of the park.

Category: Solicitation for prostitution.
Conservative state representative Bob Allen (R) was arrested on 7/11/2007 in a men's room in this park for offering to perform oral sex on an undercover policeman for $20.

*   *   *   *   *   *   *   *   *   *   *

My GPS displays NEXRAD weather. A glance at the screen showed a rapidly developing twenty mile thick area of severe weather directly ahead. There were lots of red and yellow areas displayed, which meant heavy rain and thundershowers. Even as I pulled out of the park the rain started to fall in buckets and lightning was smashing its way to the ground around me. A few minutes later I pulled under the shelter of a car wash for a few seconds to cinch up my riding suit and close the air vents in my jacket and pants. The sealed riding suit kept me dry, but was stifling in the ninety-five degree heat.

Riding in this particular storm only lasted a half hour and I was greeted on the other side with the largest rainbow I have ever seen. It was monstrous and stretched from horizon-to-horizon. This happens frequently during long-distance riding. I get hammered relentlessly by the weather and then rewarded with a spectacular show in the sky.

I planned to ride seven hours to cover the 410 miles to Key West. I timed this to be during the night so I didn't have to trail behind a line of motor homes and sightseers on the two-lane roads to the bonus. There is only one road into the Keys and the same road out, and traffic was a concern.

I'd never been to Key West, but it was offered as a bonus in every IBR. It has usually been considered a "sucker" bonus. That is, it may have looked like it was worth the time and miles but there were usually bonuses available that were worth more points for fewer miles and less aggravation. Typically, some of the riders always headed to the Keys anyway.

I worried a bit back in Spartanburg when I was making my plan as to whether it was a sucker-bonus in this rally, but I only saw two high point routes to St. Charles. They were the route to Martha's Vineyard and the one to Key West. The point value for this bonus at 1,807 points was huge and the timing from Spartanburg looked good, so south I went.

Just above Miami I made an error in routing. My GPS told me to take the toll road south around the city and I decided to save the four dollars and stay on the secondary roads. It was the wrong thing to do, as there are 600 traffic lights per mile going through Miami and it took a lot longer than I wanted to make it to South Florida.

While I was still north of the city I heard Bill Thweatt calling on the CB and found that he was right behind me. It was great to talk with another rally rider. We discussed the weather, the ride, and that we were both going to Key West. We were still following the rally guidelines of "no outside help" with routing and tried not to say anything about where we had been or where we were going past Key West.

There were problems in previous rallies with teams forming as well as non-riders possibly deciding the outcome of the rally. Mike Kneebone wanted the IBR to be an individual endeavor and special attention had been devoted to enforce this in the 2009 rulebook.

In past rallies the problem of teams had gotten out of hand in that some riders would be continually advised of the best route to follow for the highest score via cell phone by a team back at the hotel. The advent of satellite tracking devices, which some riders used, allowed these command centers to follow riders who had a real chance of winning in order to see what bonuses they may be visiting so that they could try to keep their own rider in the lead. These teams were also constantly sorting through copies of the bonus packets for alternative bonuses to visit in order to advise their rider of the highest point route.

A number of riders, myself included, felt that having a team do the heavy-lifting so that the rider could spend more time resting, or getting a higher finishing position through the help of others was cheating. We felt that the Iron Butt Rally was intended to be an individual, amateur event. The defense given by the teams was that there was no specific rule that outlawed the activity. If an action wasn't specifically forbidden in the official rules then it must be acceptable. Since the IBR organizers could not write a rule for every conceivable action, there were an infinite number of loopholes for some riders to jump through.

During the 2005 rally, several of the top riders were on their way from the start in Denver, Colorado, to a large bonus in Key West, Florida, when they were contacted via cell phone and advised by their team that they could get more points by going to Prince Edward Island on the east coast of Canada. The folks who figured this out were back in the hotel in Denver and had spent the night reviewing the bonus instructions and running various routes on computers. If a rider did not have a team, and the vast majority of riders did not, then they were at a disadvantage.

To tame the team effort in the 2007 IBR, the rally packets were printed using black ink on red paper so that they could not be photocopied or faxed. However, the black ink on red paper confusion for the teams lasted only a few hours till someone used computer filtering to copy and disperse the packets.

This did have an interesting effect on the riders. I remember quite a few times when I was stopped on the side of the road at night looking over the bonus information and trying to read the black print on red paper by the dim light of my map light. To the human eye black and red are seen as almost the same color in low light. I used some indelicate language at these times toward the riders who had caused this condition as I strained to read the instructions.

However, the team efforts continued. In the second leg of the 2007 IBR, several riders rendezvoused with a local rider near San Francisco. There were a large number of bonuses in the city, and the local rider led the group from bonus to bonus. Every rally rider had directions to these bonuses, and quite a few claimed them. However, having someone with local knowledge of the locations, traffic conditions, roads under construction, and such, gave the group an advantage over the rest of the field. Sportsmanlike conduct means different things to different people.

To try and kill the team efforts this year the riders were told that each bonus packet had a hidden identifier. If the packet made it onto the internet or into anyone else's hands other than the assigned rider, that rider could be disqualified. The USB thumb drives that we were issued with the coordinates of all of the bonuses were similarly bugged and identified.

The organizers were explicit in their discussions before this, 2009, rally about "no outside help". However, several of the riders continued to post on internet forums various loopholes that they discerned in the anti-team rules. They kept repeating the mantra that if the rules did not specifically limit or outlaw something, it was legal to do it.

In response, Lisa Landry found a simple and elegant solution. She let it be known that anything that was said or done that influenced the motion of a rider would be considered "outside help". There could be no weather reporting to the rider, no hotel or ferry reservations made by a family member or supporter, and no helpful speculation about another rider's location. Whether the rider agreed with this elimination of outside help or not, it was the Law. It worked.

Bill and I separated when he stopped for fuel as we passed through Miami just after 10:00 p.m. A few minutes later I heard him in my helmet speakers asking how things are going and I assumed that he was nearby on the CB, so I keyed my microphone and talked back but he didn't hear me, and what followed was like an Abbott and Costello routine. Bill talks to me, I talk to Bill, and we don't communicate. Then a few minutes later I heard a strange voice on the CB. It's a powerful base-station and the operator was calling for the R60 Rider on the BMW. I answer on the CB and the unknown voice says that he was trying to find me for Bill, but this faded out as I left Miami.

It turns out that Bill called me on the cell phone, which also comes through my helmet speakers. If I had simply talked back he would have heard me, but each time I keyed the microphone for the CB it killed the microphone for the cell phone. I figured this out while talking to Bill the next day. At least it was some entertainment to keep me alert as I rode along through the blackness toward Key West.

One of my chief fears while riding is hitting an animal, so I pay attention to the yellow diamond warning signs where there have been repeated animal collisions. In the east most of these signs have silhouettes of deer and in the west I've seen the signs for bear, elk, and moose. As I left the mainland I passed a few of the yellow diamond signs with the profile of a crocodile.

Then I noticed that there were openings a foot high and a few feet wide in the bottom of the concrete barriers I was riding between, and finally a warning sign to watch out for the crocodiles at the *crocodile crossings*. Holy crap! Crocodile crossings! They have openings in the road barriers so the crocodiles can get across. How long do they take to cross? Are they like deer? Do they always go straight across or can they turn and follow the road? What the heck happens if I hit one? Hitting Bambi is one bad thing but running into a reptile with a multimillion year history as a predator at the top of the food chain is another.

The ride to Key West was uneventful. It was all a two lane road with low speed limits and I couldn't see much of the surroundings for the darkness. What I did notice was that some of the Keys are huge. I had always envisioned them as little bitty islands connected by the road. My mental image of these small islands had them covered with small grass-thatched huts where folks wander about in the sun and enjoy the sound of the surf. My mental images were way off base.

They're not bitty islands; they are huge.   Some have a Walmart, Sam's Club, Target, Home Depot, and buildings the size of a large city.

The speed limits were relatively low and I had heard a lot of stories about speed traps and patrols.   I usually run at the speed limit and didn't expect any problem would arise, but I did hop on the brakes a few times when the limit dropped from 55 to 25 over the course of five feet.

The other thing I noticed was that once I got to Key West and headed for the bonus there were even more traffic lights than in Miami and they were all apparently set to turn red as I approached.

*   *   *   *   *   *   *   *   *   *   *

Sloppy Joe's bar   *1,807 points*
Anytime
Key West, Florida
Take a photo of the exterior of Sloppy Joe's bar.
Category: Public intoxication.
This was Ernest Hemingway's favorite watering hole during the time he lived in Key West with his wife and 60 cats.

*   *   *   *   *   *   *   *   *   *   *

Five riders were on the street when I pulled up and three others were heading back north. I was amazed that at 3:00 a.m. the streets were full of pedestrians moving about the bars and there were also scads of taxis shuttling them around.   Two minutes later I was retracing my path to the mainland and aiming to get off of the Key Highway by dawn and complete the 160 miles to the next bonus. If the timing worked out well, I would find a motel and get three hours of rest before continuing. I didn't want to wear myself out on the first day.

I have a bad tendency to resist stopping, for anything, once I get into the rhythm of a ride. My psyche gets set on covering miles to the exclusion of all else. I may know that I need to stop to drink, or eat, or pee, but I just keep putting the task off. Any stop, even if it only for a few minutes, makes me feel as if the ride has come to a grinding halt.

I love this kind of riding. It is cooler at night, the traffic is nonexistent, and I can just pace along with my thoughts. Frequently, I think about Susie back in Winston-Salem. Even though she relentlessly supports my riding I know that she worries. She is not a motorcycle rider, never has been. I mentioned before that she can track me with the SPOT satellite tracker, but we have both made macabre jokes that the tracker will allow her to find the body.

There are so many things that can go wrong as motorcycle riding is inherently dangerous compared to touring in a car. I can get hit by a vehicle, an animal, or suffer any number of mechanical failures. Then there are the thoughts, just below consciousness, about what can happen as we get older. What does a rider do when chest pain comes on in the middle of nowhere?

Over a decade ago Susie's brother, Keith, died in a motorcycle accident. After the funeral I asked Susie if she wanted me to stop riding. I would have given it all up if it upset her to see me leaving on rides on the motorcycle. She didn't hesitate and told me to keep on riding, but be careful. For that I'm enormously grateful.

Susie cheers me on, laughs at my stories of road craziness, and constantly pushes me toward enjoying the sport. She is my anchor when things are going badly and my shining light when things go well. But, I know that she worries.

-Day Two, Tuesday-

At 5:00 a.m. I was back on the mainland and found a motel room in Florida City to catch three hours of sleep. This took some doing because most motels apparently figure that with checkout time at 11:00 a.m., there will not be many folks who want to check in at 5:00. I got lucky and found a clerk awake at the fifth motel I tried. But, before she would rent me the room I had to convince her that I fully understood what an 11 a.m. checkout time meant and guaranteed her I would be gone by 9:00.

When I got to my room the area was shrouded in fog and I found the outside walls and door covered with small, green tree frogs. It was just another memory to file away.

After three hours of sleep I continued on with temperatures in the low 80s and a sunny sky. I was happy that my plan was holding together well, and was riding on back-roads with very little traffic. I was headed to a bonus that was at the same time tragic and bizarre. Higdon would present a lot of these as the rally progressed.

*   *   *   *   *   *   *   *   *   *   *

Miccosukee Resort   *1,525 points*
Daylight hours only
Miami, Florida
Take a photo of the dock behind the hotel with the signs —Danger Live Alligators.
Category: Attempted theft, escape.
Police responded to a call that two men were breaking into cars in the hotel's parking lot. Upon arrival they captured one suspect but another escaped and, despite signs warning of the presence of alligators, jumped into a retaining pond. He began

to swim away, but was quickly dragged under water and killed
by one of the pond's reptiles.
*   *   *   *   *   *   *   *   *   *   *

Do you cry or cringe at a place like this? I did what any IBR rider would do. I tried not to dwell on the calamity that had taken place here. I took the picture and rolled on north. Just a sixty mile ride away was Boynton Beach. The humidity was low, the temperature was pleasant, the sky was clear, and the roads were good. What more can a motorcyclist possibly ask for?

*   *   *   *   *   *   *   *   *   *   *

Winn-Dixie   *1,306 points*
Daylight hours only
Boynton Beach, Florida
Take a photo of the Charleston Mall sign.
Category: Robbery.

Lucinda Brayne, then 17 and on probation from an unrelated offense, stole $164 from a Girl Scout's cookie stand that was operating near the Winn-Dixie supermarket in this mall. Caught, she confessed, but objected when told that she'd have to return the stolen money. Asked if she were sorry, the blond said, "I'm not sorry. I'm just pissed that I got caught." Not long thereafter Brayne was arrested again for skipping out on a bill from Denny's.

*   *   *   *   *   *   *   *   *   *   *

At this bonus I ran into the type of thing that may cost a rider points at the scoring table. The instructions say take a photo of the sign that says "Charleston Mall", but the signs all say "Charleston Square". It could be a trick, it could be an oversight, or I could be at the wrong shopping center.

There are a fair number of long-distance motorcycle rallies that do have humorous themes or whose Rally Masters employ trickery. In a recent rally, riders were told to visit a location and take a photo of "the large bat", and near the target location was a humongous baseball bat. However, just down the road was an enormous bat of the flying variety. A careful reading of the bonus instructions would guide the rider to the right bat. Quite a few riders chose the wrong one.

There are no tricks in the Iron Butt Rally. The rally is about attention to detail, alertness, the ability to read and comprehend instructions, and the ability to ride a motorcycle safely over long distances. This was my reason for calling the Rally Master for clarification. Lisa told me that I was at the right place; we exchanged pleasantries and I was off to Orlando.

*   *   *   *   *   *   *   *   *   *   *

Airport   *556 points*
Daylight hours only
Blue satellite parking lot
Orlando, Florida
Take a photo of the entrance to the satellite parking lot (you do not have to enter the parking lot itself, and we will give you wide latitude on this bonus photo).
Category: Attempted murder.
Astronaut Lisa Nowack assaulted her romantic rival for the affections of a fellow astronaut early in the morning of 2/5/2007 in this satellite parking lot (near Station C in the blue lot). Nowack is a hero to many in the endurance riding community for having driven non-stop from Houston, Texas to Orlando while wearing a diaper so as to minimize bathroom stops.
*   *   *   *   *   *   *   *   *   *   *

I found the parking lot easily, took my photo, and entered my information on the bonus sheet. All the while, I was wondering if, or when, airport security might come ask what I was doing. You would think that in these days of heightened security at transportation hubs someone would wonder why over a dozen motorcyclists were stopping to take a photograph of the parking lot. Apparently no one cared.

Would I ever come here on my own? Nope. Was it entertaining to read the story in the bonus information and look around? Yep.

This is a major dividend of riding in the IBR, getting to visit places I never even thought about for a bit of entertainment. It was only 180 miles from the last bonus and now I hopped ninety miles north to Gator Joe's bar.

* * * * * * * * * * *

Gator Joe's   *418 points*
Daylight hours only
Ocklawaha, Florida
Take a photo of the exterior of Gator Joe's bar.
Category: Shootout.
In what still is the biggest shootout in FBI history, a four-hour battle with several thousand shots fired, Kate "Ma" Barker, the leader of a gang that included Alvin "Creepy" Karpis, was killed with her son on 1/16/1935 in a lakefront house just to the west of this bar.
* * * * * * * * * * *

In the parking lot I encountered a family out for dinner and "dad" asked about the bike, the GPS units, the fuel cell, and then the rally. I spent a few minutes entertaining them with details about long-distance riding, and the Iron Butt Rally, and then I asked him to take my photo. He said that he would be "tickled to do it".

I was also watching the clock because the last Florida bonus was daylight-only and a far piece away. They wished me luck and I wished them a good dinner. My next stop was the Alumni Hall in Gainsville which was a short one hour ride to the north.

*   *   *   *   *   *   *   *   *   *   *

Emerson Alumni Hall   *317 points*
Daylight hours only
Gainesville, Florida
Take a photo of the building entrance.
Category: Inciting to riot.
On 9/17/2007 at a public forum on campus Andrew Meyer was questioning Sen. John Kerry when Meyer dropped a vulgar word and his microphone was cut off. Police moved in to remove Meyer, who continued to shout and protest his

eviction. Police warned they would stun him with a Taser if he didn't calm down. Meyer then shouted, "Don't tase me, bro!," a plea that was later named by the Yale Book of Quotations as the most memorable words of 2007. They tased him anyway.

*　*　*　*　*　*　*　*　*　*　*

This bonus was on a city street that was fairly busy for 7 p.m., and I did get some mighty strange looks from the students as I walked around in the 96 degree heat in what appeared to be a snowmobile suit. I'm glad I could provide some entertainment.

Back at the bike I checked the clock and timing was tight on the last daylight-only bonus at Macclenny. I had to travel fifty-four miles and had an hour and a few minutes till sunset. That doesn't sound like a hard thing to do but most of the riding was on local roads, through small towns with low speed limits, and I had to find a bench at a cemetery.

* * * * * * * * * * *

Macedonia Cemetery   *399 points*
Daylight hours only
Macclenny, Florida
*Take a photo of the stone bench at the rear of the cemetery
(bearing the inscription "II Timothy 4: 7 & 8").*
Category: Theft.
*A woman became so upset at thieves who were stealing
flowers from her husband's grave that she installed an
infrared, motion-activated camera under a park bench that
was aimed at the gravestone. The next night the thieves stole
the camera. The case remains unsolved.*

* * * * * * * * * * *

The cemetery was located where the GPS said it would
be but there were more benches than I could count and the
light was starting to fade when I arrived. After a lot of
wandering I finally went to the exact GPS location in the bonus
listing and compared all of the benches in sight with a
photograph on the bonus sheet and found the right bench. I

grabbed the photo and could relax a bit, because the next bonus on my route was an "anytime" bonus. I had time to grab a burger before I started the push toward the checkpoint. Oh - it was also starting to rain again but it only looked like another brief one-hour shower.

Before I left the cemetery I took care of the call-in bonus. This bonus allows the IBR staff to keep some kind of track of the riders: Where they are, where they are going, and from what I can gather it also allows the staff to gauge how the rider is feeling based on how they sound. These are easy points to get as long as the rider remembers to call, calls at the right time, and gives the required information in the right sequence. It serves as a sort of an intelligence test on the fly.

* * * * * * * * * * *

Call-In Bonus - *no specific location 250 points*
Available August 25, 2009
Noon – 11:59:59 p.m. Pacific
Call xxx-xxx-xxxx and leave the following information:
Your name, your rider number, your location (city/town and state/province), the last bonus you scored, and the bonus you are headed for.
* * * * * * * * * * *

I was on-plan as I left Florida for the Georgia bonus and so far my routing had been effective. Every rider has their own particular system for routing. Some construct the entire route for a leg using a computer mapping system, transfer this to their GPS, and then follow the route turn-by-turn as their GPS instructs them. Others route on the fly based on their immediate needs.

One rider, Jim Owen, was good enough to publish the specifics of his routing strategy on-line. Jim, who came astonishingly close to winning in 2005 and again in 2007, wasn't really giving anything away in terms of his competitive edge because it is the rider that makes the rally a success or failure, not the routing methodology.

I use a combination of high and low tech for my routing. After I downloaded the bonuses to my laptop and separated them into point categories, I ran various routes through my Streets & Trips mapping program until I had a route that got me to the bonus locations at the appropriate time to score the bonus. I then confirmed this using paper maps with the bonuses highlighted to get the big picture.

Before you get the idea that a rider has to be capable of using sophisticated computer equipment and programs to ride in the Iron Butt, I would like to pass on two stories.

Eric Jewel, who is riding in this IBR, is one of the best long-distance riders around. He has had podium finishes in just about every rally that he has ridden in. I was talking to Eric one day about routing and he mentioned that until the 2007 IBR the GPS he used did not have routing capability. It was a mere moving map that showed his location and he did all of his routing by using paper maps and a calculator.

There is also the story of Rick Morrison, a rider who not only used paper maps but used a cigarette for figuring his routing distances. He knew that it was a certain amount of miles and time from one end of the cigarette to the other when placed on a map and he would reportedly move the cigarette end-over-end across the map to figure where to go. No computer programs necessary.

In my case, I used two Garmin GPSMap 478 GPS units mounted on the handlebars. I carried a backup GPS during the rally in case something happened to the main unit. One unit was always routing me from bonus to bonus and I used the other one to run alternative routes as I rode.

In addition to the map, the main unit displayed my exact speed, local time, average speed for the leg, and estimated time of arrival (ETA) to the next bonus. The backup GPS showed local sunrise and sunset times, total miles ridden for the leg, and the local time at the next checkpoint.

-Day Three, Wednesday-

The four-hundred mile ride to Armuchee was mostly interstate, mostly dark, and only took six hours. I arrived at the bonus at 2:30 in the morning and positioned the bike so that the headlights lit up the signs.

* * * * * * * * * * *

Floyd/Chattooga county line on US-27/GA-1 *646 points*
Anytime
Armuchee, Georgia
Take a photo that shows both the Chattooga County and Mile 0 signs at this location.
Category: Reckless driving, flight, improper passing, leaving the scene of an accident.
On 9/5/2007 on US-27 between Summerville and Armuchee Justin Patterson, 22, reached speeds of 154 mph on his 2002 Suzuki Hayabusa. He was trying not to be late to the Georgia State Police barracks to pick up his Class M motorcycle license.
* * * * * * * * * * *

The 'Mile 0" sign had been hit by a car and torn out of the ground, but I figured that another IBR rider had placed it next to the Chattooga sign. A few cars passed by while I was getting this bonus and I wondered what they thought of a lone motorcycle rider by the side of the road taking pictures of road signs in the dark of night.

I really enjoy riding at night. There is no traffic, temperatures in summer are cooler, and there are few distractions. I get a chance to think about life, family, the ride, and things in general. My music collection ranges from classical, to psychedelic, to jazz, and to almost everything that Frank Zappa ever put on record.

My last bonus of this leg, the Meriwether Lewis National Monument on the Natchez Trace Parkway, was the next stop. This was a four and a half hour ride over 250 miles for a large bonus. The last few miles were along the Natchez Trace Parkway, which reminded me of the Blue Ridge Parkway back home. It was a low speed limit, well laid out two lane road with what may be great scenery. I don't know about the view because I was riding in pitch darkness to get there and arrived just before dawn on Wednesday morning.

There was another rider at the monument waiting for sunrise and we ended up talking about the ride for about a half hour till the sky started to lighten. I should really have just laid down near the monument and taken a one hour nap.

*   *   *   *   *   *   *   *   *   *   *

Meriwether Lewis National Monument *1,014 points*
Daylight hours only
Natchez Trace Parkway, mile marker 386
Hohenwald, Tennessee
Take a photo of the Meriwether Lewis memorial column.
Category: Unexplained death.
Meriwether Lewis, 35, former secretary to Thomas Jefferson and co-leader of the Lewis-Clark expedition across America in 1804-06, was shot and killed here on the night of 10/10/1809, most probably by his own hand. The broken column is intended to represent a life tragically cut short.
*   *   *   *   *   *   *   *   *   *   *

At dawn we took our photos, but even as I rode away I had a gnawing suspicion that my picture looked too much like a nighttime flash picture and didn't show enough sky light to qualify for the daylight-only bonus.

There were no services or towns close by to get a computer generated receipt to prove I was there at sunrise, and I kept mulling this over as I traveled toward the main road.

Finally, after a few minutes, I turned around and went back to the monument. I was just not willing to take the chance on losing 1,014 points because the photograph didn't show proof of daylight.

By the time I got back to the monument there was more than enough light to prove that I had followed the directions in the rally pack and there were two other riders taking their photos. I was back on the bike at 6:45 and felt assured that I had these points.

The first photograph was taken at dawn. The second was
taken twenty minutes later.

I now had to ride 600 miles to the checkpoint.   A
straight-shot ride would put me in St. Charles at 4:00 p.m.,
which was five hours before the checkpoint was scheduled to
open.   To me, a five hour cushion at the checkpoint was
reasonable, especially since I was riding the 1976 R60.

To a rider who is wanting to win this rally it would be
considered a criminal waste of valuable time.   The top riders
would be pulling into the checkpoint with just minutes to spare
till the opening time of 9:00 p.m. Starting at 9:00 there were
penalty points added till the checkpoint closed at 11:00 p.m.

Some riders are more than willing to arrive at the
checkpoint during the penalty period if they feel that the
penalty will be offset by the points gained by being late. If a
rider grabs a 2,000 point bonus and this costs him 500 points
in penalties for being late, there would be a net gain of 1,500

points, and for those riders who stand a real chance of winning this IBR, that would be a fair trade.

*   *   *   *   *   *   *   *   *   *   *

Time penalty begins 9:00:01 p.m.   After 9:00:00 p.m. there will be a 10-point per minute penalty for being late.   Any rider who arrives after 11:00:00 p.m. (beginning at 11:00:01 p.m.) will not be considered a finisher of the rally.

*   *   *   *   *   *   *   *   *   *   *

No quarter is given in the Iron Butt for lateness at a checkpoint.   Popular excuses such as bad weather, heavy traffic, a flat tire, a motorcycle problem, running out of gas, or the bridge-is-out are not acceptable. There are no excuses. A rider either makes it to the checkpoint on time or doesn't. This is not called the World's Toughest Motorcycle Competition for nothing.

Speaking of traffic.   Nashville, Tennessee, was a parking lot at 7:45 on Wednesday morning even though I was on the beltway.   Truckers on the CB said that this was just part of driving around Nashville.   One referred to it with a smile in his voice as "the Nashville experience".   I hated creeping along at a snail's pace and it took the better part of an hour to clear the city from south to north. From this point on I encountered fine riding conditions toward the checkpoint.

As I approached St. Charles I decided to forgo any other bonuses and get in to the checkpoint for early scoring. I was not trying to win this rally; my goal was to be an official finisher and to cross the finish line grinning like a fool. After scoring I would check over the BMW and then get as much sleep as I could before the next bonus packet was handed out at 4:00 a.m. Thursday.

I pulled into the parking lot in St. Charles right at 5:00 p.m. and was greeted by IBR staff and well-wishers and it was raining again. It seems that every evening on this rally was a wet one. But this was a gentle soaking rain instead of a gully-washer.

Voni Glaves, a veteran of the 2003 IBR and a rider who once won a mileage contest by riding over 73,000 miles in just six months, was there to greet arriving riders just as she did at the checkpoint in 2007.

Grinning in St. Charles (Photo by Voni Glaves)

You can't miss Voni, as she is always smiling, always dressed head to toe in red, and is usually carrying a camera so she can take photos of the riders and then e-mail them to the folks back home. She knew that we riders were weary and she also knew that a smiling face, a hug, and a few kind words could do wonders to lift the spirits.

I entered the scoring area and showed my identification card to officially check in. Ira Agins was running the check-in desk and stopped the clock on my rally leg even as he started another timer for scoring. I had a two hour limit to get my bonus materials together and return to be scored. I then headed to my room to get my documentation together.

On the way there Ben Hutchens, a friend from work, called to congratulate me on making the first checkpoint. He had been tracking my progress on the SPOT web page. The call temporarily reminded me that there was more going on in the world than just the IBR. But just temporarily.

Once scoring begins, the rider can't leave the scoring table to retrieve missing paperwork or receipts. This rally is not just about riding around the continent, or even being able to route efficiently through the bonus listing. It includes being able to present your proof of performance in an indisputable fashion. Needless to say, scoring is a bug-a-boo for a lot of riders because there is only one chance to get it right or wrong.

In previous IBRs we used Polaroid photos to document bonuses. However, Polaroid stopped making the film for their instant cameras last year and this is the first IBR to use digital photos. The memory card from a rider's camera had to be inspected before scoring to make sure that no one falsified their images. Point penalties, the loss of the bonus, or possible disqualification awaited anyone who ran afoul of the inspection. Before sitting at the scoring table, each rider had to meet with either Bill Shaw or Dave McQueeney to download our bonus photos.

Every volunteer that helped make the IBR a success is a devoted long-distance rider. There are two items that stand out about Dave McQueeney. He has ridden and documented over one million miles on BMW motorcycles and he has ridden the Four Corners Motorcycle Tour.

To certify the Four Corners Tour the rider has to visit four remote corners of the U.S. They are San Ysidro, California; Blaine, Washington; Madawaska, Maine; and Key West, Florida, and finish within three weeks. They can do it in any order and they document the visit with a post card and photograph. For most motorcyclists this is done in a circle around the country and is a monumental, once-in-a-lifetime achievement.

McQueeney rode from his home in California to San Ysidro and then returned home. He changed motorcycles and rolled on to Blaine and then home again. On a third motorcycle he went to Madawaska and home yet again. On a fourth motorcycle he rode to Key West and then home. He did all of this within the time limit by staying in the saddle hour-after-hour and completing sixteen 1,000 mile days in a row. I stand in awe of riders like Dave.

Eddie James was my scorer and he meticulously scanned my paperwork. My fuel receipts were in order and correct. My fuel log matched the receipts and the fuel usage and mileage agreed with where I claimed to have visited. The bonus sheet information was filled out correctly and matched the photos used for verification and the flag was in each photo. Even though Eddie has ridden in five IBRs, he was still checking my information against a rule sheet that each scorer used and he mentioned that this was his first time scoring "for these folks" and he wanted to do it right.

In the 2007 IBR I had a problem at the checkpoint and at the finish, as I lost a small amount of points for just plain stupid mistakes. Both times I had the correct information on my receipts but wrote something different on the score sheet. This time I didn't leave any points on the table and scored 11,241 points for the leg. The number used as a guide for finisher status at the end of the rally was 9,000 for this leg, so I was ahead of the game. At least for now.

Next stop was the parking lot where I checked the engine valve clearances on the R60. Because the cylinder heads and valves had been rebuilt in May and I only had 12,000 miles on them, I wanted to check them for tightness at each checkpoint. Too tight a clearance and there would be engine damage, too loose and the engine would not run efficiently.

The valve check involves removing covers on the engine and using a set of feeler gauges, calibrated strips of metal about the thickness of a hair, to measure the opening between parts. This only took ten minutes but involved sitting on the rain soaked parking lot.

It brought back memories of servicing the BMW at the checkpoint during the 2007 IBR. That parking lot wasn't just rain soaked; it was the target of a line of severe thundershowers that was moving through Saint Louis, and I changed the rear tire as well as checked the valves and the carburetors while a helpful onlooker held an umbrella over me during the downpour.

The valves' clearances were spot-on and the plugs looked perfect. I topped off the engine oil with one of the three quarts I had sent ahead to the checkpoint and topped off the air in the front tire with an air compressor I carried on the cycle. That meant that the BMW was ready for the second leg.

Finally, I went to my room to get what sleep I could before the second leg bonus packets would be handed out at 4:00 a.m. Thursday.

7 Leg Two – St. Charles to Santa Ana

-Day Four, Thursday-

At four in the morning we were to gather in the same room where scoring had taken place the night before. It was raining off and on and the humidity was hovering around 620%. I spent a few minutes getting all of my gear secured to the bike, except what was needed for routing the next leg. I turned both GPS units on, sent an "I'm OK" message on the SPOT satellite tracker, and did a walk-around the BMW to make sure everything looked in place.

Back in the room I had paper maps for half a dozen states opened on the bed, the computer was on and open to my mapping program; a calculator, scrap paper, and high-lighters were at the ready. I also had checked the weather for the western half of the country and it seemed like the rain would clear after a while, but there were forecasts of thunder showers for this evening.

It turns out that my thoughts yesterday of getting to the checkpoint early so that I could get a good night's sleep had been for the best. Quite a few riders had gotten in just before the checkpoint closed and some had been going through the scoring process until 2:00 a.m. This left them almost no time for sleep before having to deal with the bonus packet for the second leg and get riding.

The bonus packet for the first leg was handed out sixteen hours before the start of the leg. We had time to work through the bonuses and tightly plan our first leg. The packets for the second and third legs were handed out with the rally clock ticking. The longer a rider spent planning these legs the less time there was for riding.

At the beginning of the meeting Mike Kneebone read off the top ten riders' names and their points.

Position	Rider	Points
First	Jeff Earls	16629
Second	Jim Owen	16331
Third	Derek Dickson	16143
Fourth	Andy Mills	15653
Fifth	Eric Jewell	15076
Sixth	Greg Marbach	15028
Seventh	Roger Sinclair	14726
Eighth	Mike Hutsal	14447
Ninth	Chris Sakala	14181
Tenth	Alan Barbic	14141

Jeff Earls was in first place even though he had lost his rally-flag on the very first day. Losing his flag meant that he had to have his face appear in every bonus photo. Jim Owen, who almost won in 2005 and 2007, was second. Now the average rider in the room looked worn, weary, rough, and in some cases disheveled. Jim was standing next to me, sipping from a cup of coffee, barefoot, and looking totally rested, calm, and ready to ride.

As the point totals for the top ten were recited it was interesting to look around the room and see the response on riders' faces. Some of the rookies seemed shocked at the high values. A few riders sighed as they realized just how high the bar was being set. Most of the top ten riders just stood there waiting for the bonus packets, as they were now given a good idea of how the competition was shaking out. As for me, I mentioned to Jim that I hadn't seen a route with nearly 16,000 points on the leg. He just smiled.

At 4:10 the bonus packets for the second leg were handed out, everyone was admonished to ride safely, and the second leg was on. I did stop for a second to check the posted standings and noted that I had 11,241 points and was 43rd. Wah-hoo!

Twenty-seven riders had not made enough points to be considered finishers. This in no way meant that they were out of the rally. What it did mean was that they would have to be very careful in planning the next two legs and be able to successfully execute their plan. As the rally goes on, the point values increase and the first leg is usually never an indicator of how the final standings will shape up.

The next checkpoint was Santa Ana, California, which is outside of Los Angeles. I had eighty-nine hours, or roughly three and a half days, from when the bonus packets were handed out until the opening of the checkpoint. After studying the offerings I decided to head to a large bonus in north-central Iowa, then down to two large bonuses in southern Mississippi, and finally west to pick up some smaller bonuses on the way to the checkpoint.

This is a good place to discuss what may be the most divisive word in the long-distance riding community and the word that is most misunderstood by folks who are not familiar with the IBR. That word is "race". People who hear about the length of the rally in both time and miles assume that the riders are racing each other to the finish. Nothing could be farther from the truth.

The Iron Butt Rally is just that - a rally. It is a test of skill in reading, understanding, routing through a large selection of bonus listings, and endurance riding. It is the challenge of moving through the eleven days no matter the weather, the road conditions, the rider's health, or spirits. Getting to the checkpoints or the finish first earns a rider absolutely nothing. And yet the mistaken idea that this is a race lingers on.

Let's look at this another way. Fatigue management is a critical part of a rider's success or failure in long-distance riding. At higher speeds a rider has to scan the traffic patterns more often and be computing the distances between themselves and other vehicles more frequently. This may not make a difference on a one or two hour ride for the average rider, but long-distance riding is not your everyday ride. In the IBR I was in the saddle for 18 or 19 hours a day and anything that would jack up the level of fatigue, even a little bit, would lead to my inability to cover the hours and miles needed to complete the rally.

There is an understanding in the long-distance community that having good reading comprehension is better than half the battle of succeeding in a rally. As I set up a route for this leg I thought that I had carefully read all of the bonus information, but apparently I had a brain-fart when I looked at a bonus in Fort Smith, Arkansas. It was for a massive, 4,235 points if the rider would visit a former house of ill-repute and take a one hour tour. This would have fit in nicely with my route and would have yielded considerably more points-per-mile-ridden than the route I followed through Mississippi.

As I went through the listings I misread this bonus location as being in Oklahoma instead of Arkansas and had mentally set it aside as not on my prime route. Second guessing oneself is never a good thing, but looking back on the route for the second leg I am continually amazed at how I missed the Fort Smith bonus knowing now what a difference it would have made in the leg in terms of points and miles ridden.

I left St. Charles just after 7:00 a.m. for the 378 mile, six hour ride to the National Hobo Museum. As I was riding at my slow-but-steady pace toward the interstate, I was passed by fellow rider Richard Buber. A few minutes later he passed me again. Then five minutes later here he comes by me for the third time and I've got a grin on my face. A mile up the road I pass him as he is stopped on the shoulder looking through his rear trunk, and in my mirror I can see him get back on the bike and soon he comes around me again.

Finally, as we approach the entrance to the toll road Richard stops at the sign that says *exact change or I PASS tag only*, does a U-turn, and heads back south. I'm guessing that he doesn't have change or the toll tag, but since the only big bonus in this direction is the museum, I rightly guess that he will pass me at least one more time this morning.

The only other event worth noting on the way north to the museum was seeing Rick Miller riding southbound, obviously returning from the museum when I was still an hour from the bonus. Turns out Rick had plotted the major bonuses and left the checkpoint over an hour before I had.

I could have felt discouraged to be behind Rick and started second-guessing my plan, but I learned in the 2007 IBR that once I had a route I should stick with it and not let the sight or the thoughts of another rider cause me to challenge my thinking. So I didn't fret about Rick being "ahead" of me and just motored on.

The ability to puzzle out the rally packet and successfully ride your plan leads to the highest point score and that is what determines the standings. Riding a 1976 motorcycle with a top speed approaching some of the speed limits on western roads has given me an insight into making miles. It is the ability to stay in the saddle and ride that makes miles add up.

Fast gas stops, bathroom stops, and food stops equate to more time riding. Eric Jewell, who was riding his fourth IBR, once told me that going through the drive-thru at a burger restaurant makes for the fastest meal breaks. I tried his tip during this rally and it worked well. I would pull up to the serving window and get a couple of hamburgers, unwrap them, and place them in the dog-dish that rests on top of my fairing. It was sometimes messy but always quick.

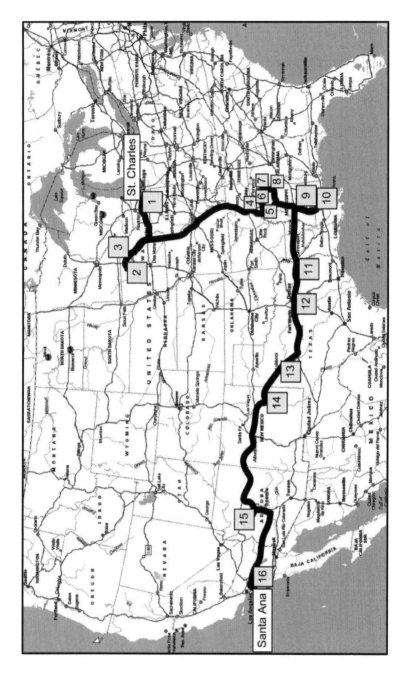

The second leg

As I arrived at the Hobo museum there were four other riders out front. They were hubbubing that the bonus was closed with a note on the door saying that it will open late that day. No hubbub was needed as the IBR rules cover just such a problem.

*   *   *   *   *   *   *   *   *   *   *

National Hobo Museum   *4,013 points*
10:00am - 5:00pm
Britt, Iowa
Obtain a stew card.
Category: Vagrancy.
For most of American history vagrancy was a status that could lead to immediate arrest and incarceration. This museum celebrates that almost forgotten lifestyle.

*   *   *   *   *   *   *   *   *   *   *

I took a photo of the door with the note and my flag and headed out to get a local receipt with a time stamp and location to show I was there.

The next planned stop was a bonus with such a low value that I usually wouldn't even think about stopping. But, it was only twenty-three miles away and on a direct route back to the main road.

*   *   *   *   *   *   *   *   *   *   *

Surf Ballroom   *47 points*
Anytime
Clear Lake, Iowa
Take a photo of the exterior of the Surf Ballroom building.
Category: Negligent homicide.
Buddy Holly's last gig was here on the night of 2/2/1959. The plane in which he, Ritchie Valens, J. P. ("The Big Bopper") Richardson, and the pilot crashed took off from the Mason City airport a few miles to the east of here. Valens won a coin toss for the last seat with a then unknown guitarist, Waylon Jennings, for the last seat in the plane.
*   *   *   *   *   *   *   *   *   *   *

This was a very quick bonus to grab and I was in and out in less than a minute. My next bonus was in Memphis, Tennessee, 697 miles and eleven hours southeast. I figured that my estimated time of arrival was 7:00 Friday morning and I expected a long but uneventful ride. I expected wrongly.

As I headed south my weather radar showed a group of serious thundershowers forming between Iowa and Missouri, but the band of weather ran east to west and was only fifteen miles thick. I reckoned that I could punch through the rain in fifteen or twenty minutes.

As the afternoon progressed the band of storms got thicker and the orange to ocher colors showed extreme rain in the center. I became resigned to the idea that I was going to be traveling through a mass of bad weather, and just as the sun set I fueled up and got my riding suit secure for the downpour.

Did I write "downpour"? I meant a gully-washing cloudbursting frog-strangling drenching. The wind wasn't bad at all but the rain was unending and at times felt as if it was a solid sheet of water coming down instead of a mass of drops. The storms shifted from east to west into a north to south pattern and I was riding north to south. It now appeared that I would be in this aquarium for three or four hours instead of fifteen or twenty minutes.

The reality of the Iron Butt Rally is that if you're heading for a bonus, the weather doesn't matter. Sure the rider will get drenched, or hammered by the wind, or sunbaked and blistered riding through hours of splintered-sunlight, but the bonus is the goal.

This night I was riding through such relentless rain that it was running down the inside of my helmet visor, which actually helped wash the humidity-induced fog clear from the inside. A redeeming factor was that the state road I was following in Missouri was built like an Interstate highway back east; four lanes, divided with a high speed limit. However, local driveways and cross-streets connected directly to the road.

Usually, as long as I keep moving on the motorcycle the rain is flung over my head by the windshield. Not tonight.

Just after dark I had to stop twice in less than an hour to clear the inside of my face shield because rain forced its way between the shield and my anti-fog insert and it was beginning to get hard to see. The insert was a specially made piece of plastic which fit on the inside and against the main face shield and was supposed to keep fog from forming and promote good visibility. I finally just removed this high-tech insert and that cured the problem.

No more fogging, no vision problems - just the nagging thought about how much I had paid for that fine piece of technology that I now realized was unnecessary.

When the rain finally fell to my rear near midnight, I stopped in a city called Festus.

-Day Five, Friday-

I got three hours of truly needed sleep and then rolled out toward Memphis. Putting on the soggy riding suit and helmet that morning was a miserable reminder of the wet ride the night before, but I knew that it would dry in the morning wind. Besides, I had no other choice.

The persistent pain in my left big toe where the boot lining was failing was a reminder of another sort. This one was about the nature of the IBR where the rider has to suck it up and continue on no matter what.

* * * * * * * * * * *

Lorraine Motel   *654 points*
Anytime
Memphis, Tennessee
Take a photo of the "Lorraine Motel" sign.
Category: Assassination.
Civil rights leader Martin Luther King, Jr. was shot and killed on the balcony of this motel on 4/4/1968. It is now a civil rights museum.
* * * * * * * * * * *

I shared a few words with the three riders I saw at the bonus and with a young woman who was selling Martin Luther King Jr. memorabilia. I also spent a few moments thinking about the tragedy that happened at such a mundane place and how it changed history. However, I was in the middle of the IBR and those last moments were spent while riding.

It was time to move on toward a series of bonuses in Mississippi. I was going to make a loop of northern Mississippi and end the day at a bonus that is the home of the winner of the 2005 rally.   My next bonus was a short, hour and a half ride to Sumner, Mississippi, just ninety-six miles to the south over mostly two lane, lightly traveled back roads.

*   *   *   *   *   *   *   *   *   *   *

Courthouse   *539 points*
Anytime
Sumner, Mississippi
Take a photo of the historical marker on the courthouse grounds that memorialize the murder trial.
Category: Race murder.
Emmett Till, an African-American teenager from Chicago who had been visiting relatives near here in the summer of 1955, made a suggestive remark to the wife of a convenience store owner in Money, Mississippi.   He was dragged from his uncle's home by the wife's husband and brother-in-law, beaten, killed, and thrown into the Tallahatchie River.   The killers were tried and acquitted in this courthouse.   They later confessed to the murder in an article in Look magazine after being paid $4,000.
*   *   *   *   *   *   *   *   *   *   *

Bob Higdon did a fine job of finding bonus locations. Some were funny, some entertaining, some educational, and some were just plain tragic. This was one of the latter. There is time while riding between bonuses to think about what I had just learned or seen. Sometimes there is a bit too much time.

The ride itself was going well. I had dried out from last night's rain and the current temperatures were in the low nineties. Actually, all of Mississippi was a good ride. It was hot and humid, but bearable, as long as I was moving along.

I didn't feel tired and was certain that I was a ahead of the time, speed, and distance curve for this leg. The next bonus in Oxford was seventy miles and an hour and a half away. Most of the riding was through small towns, on secondary roads, and traffic was light. I was making good time. Until...

*   *   *   *   *   *   *   *   *   *   *

Sculpture of James Meredith   *611 points*
Anytime
Oxford, Mississippi
Take a photo of the sculpture of Meredith from any angle. Either your bike or your flag must be in the photo. If you use the flag, do NOT place it on the sculpture.
Category: Race riot.
A riot during James Meredith's attempt to be the first African-American admitted to the University of Mississippi in September 1962 resulted in one death and numerous injuries.
*   *   *   *   *   *   *   *   *   *   *

This bonus was deep in a University campus and I arrived smack in the middle of class-change. I had to sit at crosswalks that always seemed to have at least one person in them as my "average-speed" displayed on my GPS dropped like a rock. In most locales if there is a pedestrian in a crosswalk it is illegal to proceed through the crossing. I wasn't sure if that law was in effect here, but I wasn't taking any chances.

If I was paranoid I would believe that the students were timing their crossing so the walk would always be occupied. But it was just chance that put me in a position that

I would be creeping at a snail's pace in the ninety-plus degree heat and humidity. Every minute getting to the bonus and back to the open road added a bit of misery to the ride.

It took me almost thirty minutes to get two tenths of a mile to the statue, wait for a clear shot for the photo, and escape. Interestingly enough, not one of the kids on this campus gave a second look at the motorcycle rider in the full black riding suit standing in their midst with a camera.

It was then on to Tupelo and the boyhood home of Elvis. I was thankful to be back on the open road and out of the Oxford traffic. This was a short hop at only fifty miles. I was still on schedule and feeling good.

*   *   *   *   *   *   *   *   *   *   *

Elvis Presley's boyhood home   *458 points*
Daylight hours only
Tupelo, Mississippi
Take a photo of the front of the house from the street.
Category: Uttering a false instrument.

Elvis Presley's father Vernon, who built this house, was imprisoned in Mississippi's notorious Parchman prison from 6/1/1938 until 2/6/1939 for altering a $4 check to read $14.

*   *   *   *   *   *   *   *   *   *   *

It took less than a minute to take the photo of the small house and log the bonus information, and then I rode on toward an "Anytime" bonus in West Point, forty-seven miles due south on a nice country road. Did I mention that I love riding?

*   *   *   *   *   *   *   *   *   *   *

Holiday Inn Express   *251 points*
Anytime
West Point, Mississippi
Take a photo of the front of motel including the mailbox that shows the "1190" address indicator.
Category: Disturbing the peace.

In December 2006 Barnham Bailey was fined $279 for tossing a 60-pound pig over the motel's counter. He is also implicated in three other late night animal-tossing incidents in town — a smaller pig and two opossums. None of the animals had been hurt, though they may have been somewhat embarrassed.

*   *   *   *   *   *   *   *   *   *   *

     Now on to Shane Smith's house in McComb. This was a short ride on Mississippi 82 and then 250 miles on Interstate 55. I was constantly checking time, distance, and speed. When riding at my set speed I was a happy camper. When I was stuck in traffic or moving at a snail's-pace, as in Oxford, I was sometimes in a near panic.

     Every minute of every day the IBR rider is focused on time, distance, and speed. Every bonus, every checkpoint, every rest stop is based on this focus. I was constantly running the numbers in my mind and on the backup GPS. Could I stay with my plan? Would I have to drop a bonus? Could I add a bonus? This is not just a process of worry or uncertainty. This is "the" process of succeeding in the IBR-constantly tweaking the plan, or not.

I just simply can't describe how this constant re-figuring can wreak havoc with one's normal way of doing things. Every action, fuel stop, rest break, bonus confirmation, and meal revolved around the rally. I did this constantly while awake and bet that I did it in my dreams. It becomes second-nature to be counting down the time left for a meal break as I ate, to curse a slow gas pump, or feel great that a road could be traveled more quickly than I'd thought.

Shane Smith's home was a large bonus with a one hour layover and it was only available for twelve hours. It was scheduled to start at 5:00 p.m. and the three and a half hour ride will get me to the bonus just a half hour after it opened.

*   *   *   *   *   *   *   *   *   *   *

Shane Smith's house   *4,145 points*
See requirements below
McComb, Mississippi
Spend a minimum of one hour asking the 2005 Iron Butt Rally winner why he isn't defending his title these days. This bonus will be open for 12 hours from 5:00 p.m. on Friday, August 28 until 5:00 a.m. on Saturday, August 29.
To fulfill this bonus you MUST arrive no later than 4:00 a.m..
Category: Unexplained retirement.
*   *   *   *   *   *   *   *   *   *   *

Shane is one of the most pleasant folks you can ever hope to meet. He has to be in order to open his house to a mass of malodorous, sweaty, deranged, and bedraggled motorcycle riders who look like they would be better off being committed to state-care for their own wellbeing rather than invited in for a visit.

Shane met me in his driveway to sign me in for the start of the bonus. As we talked, a couple of folks cleaned out my water jug and filled it with fresh ice and water. They offered to clean the windshield, supply anything I had lost or needed, and wished me well. It was the IBR equivalent of a NASCAR pit stop.

Shane and the gang had a spread of fruit, burgers, beverages, and other food, but all I was looking forward to was a one hour nap during the layover. I was escorted to a quiet room with four sleeping bags and air mattresses on the floor and told that they would wake me in one hour. I just wish that the smell of the burgers hadn't wafted into the room with me.

During a rally and on long rides I have a regimen that I follow when it comes to eating that is partly based on experience and partly on an article that LD rider, and former Surgeon General of the Navy, Don Arthur penned on fatigue management and long-distance motorcycle riding that appeared in the first issue of the *Iron Butt Magazine*. I found that eating carbohydrates and fats in small amounts over the course of a ride would keep my energy level up but not make me sleepy.

I usually eat two Burger King hamburgers and have a Coke-type drink about every six hours. At Shane's, I knew that if I sat down and ate any of the great smelling food waiting in his garage that in just a few hours I would be feeling the nods and have to stop long before I had planned.

I was awakened exactly one hour after I arrived at the bonus and I had Shane sign me out. The next stop was another large point bonus and it was only twenty miles to the south.

*   *   *   *   *   *   *   *   *   *   *

Nyla's Burger Basket   *3,647 points*
Anytime
Osyka, Mississippi
Take a photo of the sign identifying the building as Nyla's Burger Basket.
Category: Child neglect.
Britney Spears may not be your idea of Mom of the Year, but she's a hero in this neck of the woods. Nyla's is Britney's favorite restaurant when she's not on the road.
*   *   *   *   *   *   *   *   *   *   *

At Nyla's I stopped for a minute to explain the IBR to several folks who were standing in front of the restaurant and wondering why the motorcyclists were stopping, taking a picture, and leaving without getting a burger.

One little girl repeatedly asked "why" as I ran through my quick summary of the rally. I just smiled and told her it was an adventure and I was having fun and then I headed back north. The next bonus was near Dallas, Texas, 494 miles and eight hours away. My plan included a stop for sleep somewhere in Louisiana after I had covered a few hundred miles.

The stretch of I-55 between Nyla's and I-20 rivals anything that North Carolina (which used to be called the "Good Roads State") has to offer. I rode mile after mile of hammering misaligned concrete pavement, large potholes, slab joints vast enough to swallow an economy car, and sections that seem to be covered in loose gravel. Rarely on a paved road have I been shaken so badly. The conditions on this stretch of road will raise its ugly head later this leg.

I decided to stop in Vicksburg, Mississippi, for a few hours rest. This would be a breeze. The leg was going well, I was on schedule, and feeling good though a bit weary. I was really looking forward to this rest break.

I registered for a room but when I got back on the R60 to move the bike from the lobby area to a parking place, I felt the cycle settle a bit to the left as I swung my leg over the saddle. It felt almost as if the side-stand was sinking a small amount into dirt or asphalt. Trouble was, the driveway was solid concrete. I've ridden this bike for thirty-three years and this is not something I've ever felt before.

I got off and looked the bike over and everything was as it should be, so I got on again and the bike sickeningly shifted just a wee bit more to the left. Something was seriously wrong.

The stand that the motorcycle normally rests on is called a side-stand. This holds the bike at an angle slightly to the left of center and folds up against the frame when the cycle is ridden. On my R60 this side-stand is welded to the left foot-peg. The BMW also has a center-stand which holds the bike perfectly upright. The side-stand is easier to deploy and fold during normal riding and the center-stand is usually used for maintenance.

I put the bike on the center-stand and reached down with my right hand to grab the left foot-peg and lifted it very gently. The foot-peg and side-stand, which are made of three-quarter-inch thick steel, broke off in my hand. The thirty-three year old weld used to attach the peg assembly to the piece that bolts to the bike had failed.

I was almighty tired, the room was paid for and waiting, I was less than one third the way through this leg, I was standing in a dark parking lot holding my side-stand and foot-peg in my hand, and the clock was ticking loudly. Crap! I can't ride the motorcycle without a foot-peg and it will be a real hassle to try and ride without a side-stand. It's near midnight on a Friday night. No dealer will stock a foot-peg for a thirty three year old bike and it will take days to get one from Boxerworks, and then it would have to be altered to match my after-market side-stand. I couldn't afford the time. I couldn't afford any time at all. Gads, I was tired.

I carry a saddlebag full of spare parts. There are spare throttle, clutch, and brake cables. I have replacement connectors for every electrical part on the bike as well as a spare charging system. I have spare ignition modules and a spare coil and spark plug wire. I even packed spare front and rear inner tubes plus a tube patch kit. I carry epoxy, instant-glue, duct tape, hose clamps, and baling wire for roadside repairs. None of it would work on this failure. I was quickly getting frazzled and thinking that any time lost tonight will mean another DNF.

I called Lisa Landry to see if a clearer mind could help. I also wanted to get the number for Bob Wooldridge, a BMW motorcycle dealer, who was helping arrange for any needed repairs for riders. Lisa gets hundreds of calls from riders through the course of each IBR. As the Rally Master she makes decisions concerning missing or incorrect bonus information and talks to riders who are in accidents, missing equipment, in need of guidance, and some who just love pestering her.

When Lisa answered I dejectedly laid out my staggering tale of woe to which she brightly replied "Oh, that doesn't sound too bad. All you need is a welder." I very quietly thanked her and hung up, chagrined that I hadn't seen that all I really needed was a welder. I was wearier than I thought.

I called AAA road service, truck-stops, garages, repair centers, the highway patrol, the county Sheriff, and the police, trying to find a welder who could come out to the hotel or who I could visit via a cab at this time of night. I told each person I reached about the IBR and that I absolutely had to have the repair done as soon as possible. I even tried to find a store where I could buy a welder. No help was available anywhere.

Then, as I was standing by the hotel desk feeling disheartened and dejected with the weight of another DNF settling heavily on my shoulders, I received a call from AAA Road service. While AAA did not have a welder available, the dispatcher had found the number for a mobile twenty-four hour welding service. He had called the owner and given him my name and phone number and I should receive a call shortly. I thanked the AAA dispatcher profusely for going the extra mile.

In less than five minutes I was talking with Jonathan Sanch, the owner of a local mobile welding service, and was told that as soon as he finished with a tractor trailer he was working on fifty miles away he would come to the hotel and give me a call. I went to my room to try and get what sleep I could.

Two hours later my cell phone rang and I found that Jonathan and his mobile shop had arrived. When I got down to the dimly lit parking lot it was half empty, and there was only the occasional grunt of a truck moving along the nearby Interstate to break the silence. It was a miserable Mississippi night as the temperature hovered above eighty-seven degrees and the humidity was near one-hundred per cent. Other than the insects flying around the pole-lights there was no evidence that anyone, or anything, other than he and I, were awake. I didn't even see anyone at the hotel desk when I walked by the locked office.

As I approached the BMW Jonathan turned on his work lights and suddenly the bike and the back of his truck were bathed in daylight. His truck was equipped with several welders sized from what was needed for small precision work, to that used for joining massive sections of steel on a bridge. He had acetylene torches, power tools, a hydraulic press, and a huge assortment of aluminum and steel to use for repairs.

I handed him the footpeg assembly and showed him how it used to attach to my motorcycle. His response was eerily similar to Lisa Landry's. "Not a problem. I should have this done in a half an hour."

It was surreal to stand in that parking lot in the middle of the night, surrounded by sleeping guests, while chatting about the Iron Butt Rally with a twenty-something mechanic. He had never heard of the event and asked a lot of questions as he worked on the repair. I wondered what he thought about the short biker with a five day growth of beard, wearing what looked like black long-johns, blathering away in the deserted parking lot about riding 11,000 miles in eleven days. I have a feeling that this service call broke the monotony of his daily routine.

It took him about thirty minutes to grind the parts to a perfect fit and then weld a bead of molten metal around the break to join the two sections into one solid piece of steel.

After we fit the assembly to the R60 a half a dozen times to make sure that the angles were correct, he applied a coat of black paint and handed me the repaired part. Actually, what he handed me was the ability to continue the IBR.

The re-welded side-stand foot peg assembly.

I handed him a fair-sized amount of cash. In reality it was cheap for the time and effort that he put into the work and the fact that without his skills, my IBR would be over. As he killed his work lights and the parking lot returned to semi-darkness I shook his hand and thanked him for saving my rally. He wished me good luck on the ride and headed south toward a stranded trucker who needed a roadside repair.

Talk about an emotional roller coaster and gut wrenching changes in my mindset. In the past several hours I had hit rock bottom and then sprung back to the best of spirits. The unforeseen failure had been repaired and it was time to get back on the road.

-Day Six, Saturday –

I had gotten only two hours sleep, but I had a good-as-new weld on the foot-peg, and was heading west on I-20 for a bonus in Dallas.   In IBR terms this was a short, straightforward hop of only 360 miles, all on the Interstate.

The debacle of the night before was fading from memory. Looking back on what happened with the foot-peg, I had actually come away from the incident in good stead. The foot-peg could have broken off while I was riding and been lost on the highway. It could have given way while on the side-stand and let the bike fall over. It could have happened at a considerably worse time and in the middle of nowhere.   It could have fallen off and gotten jammed in the rear wheel.

I didn't feel lucky that it had broken off, but I knew that I was incredibly fortunate that I was stopped at a hotel, Lisa had the good grace to point out the obvious, the AAA dispatcher had decided to do a bit more research when he didn't have to, and that there happened to be a mobile welding service near Vicksburg.

The first half of the ride to Dallas went well with temperatures in the low nineties and the humidity was slowly dropping. The R60 was moving along nicely and getting forty-six miles per gallon tank after tank. The engine modifications that Boxerworks performed for the rally were spot-on and the extra ten horsepower made the bike feel much more responsive than before.

Just inside the Texas border on Interstate 20 I passed a pickup truck and the driver looked over at me and nodded and I nodded back. I pulled back into the right lane and the pickup started to pull around me in the fast lane. As I looked over, the driver was pointing down and back at my bike and shaking his head from side to side. That's not something that a rider ever wants to see, so I looked down to the left rear and everything looked just fine. I looked down to the right rear and the saddlebag was off of the bike and dragging along the road by a very small piece of sheet metal.

I slowed down carefully so I didn't dislodge the bag and then pulled off of the side of the Interstate in the grass as even in the midst of a major malfunction the comedy began.

It seemed that when we re-welded the foot-peg last night, the angle of the side-stand was just the slightest bit "off" and the bike stood more upright than it used to. This was not a major problem in the hotel parking lot and I knew I could adjust the angle if I needed to.

Well, I desperately needed to. I could not get off of the bike to check out the saddlebag due to the lay of the land and the change in side-stand angle. The stand was holding the bike straight upright and it would fall over if I got off. I rolled back and forth, I tried to sink the side-stand in the dirt, I tried shifting weight, all while dragging the saddlebag around and nothing worked. With my stubby legs I could not get off of the bike unless it was on the side-stand, and I was laughing at how ridiculous this was on the side of a busy Interstate highway.

I ended up parking perpendicular to the road with the front tire up on the pavement and the back tire in the ditch and I could finally get off of the bike. The jouncing on I-55 the night before had torn the mounting bolts for the right saddlebag through the fiberglass and the bag had fallen off. The good news was that I didn't lose the bag with all of my gear. It had apparently been dragging for quite a while, as there was a hole worn in one corner.

I was staring at the second major mishap in less than eight hours and felt just a bit stunned. I couldn't see the simple answer to this problem. I called my wife, Susie, as I figured out what to do and I did a really dumb thing.

Every rider in the IBR learns that no matter how much the family at home supports the idea of riding in the rally, there is still a lot of nervousness about what can happen during an 11 day 11,000 mile ride. Susie has been my long-distance riding cheerleader from the start. She doesn't ride but encourages me every step of the way. She does worry a lot about what can happen on the road close to home or far away and I try to keep her up to date on where I am and how I'm doing.

My wife answered the phone and the first thing I said was "I'm fucked". Even as I said it I realized she may be thinking that I've been in an accident and am injured. It was the wrong thing to say. I apologized immediately and explained that the saddlebag fell off of the bike.

She asked if I can backtrack to find it. Well, I explained that it was still with me and I've got to figure how to reattach the thing and Susie's reply was "Don't you have duct tape, or rope, or wire? Stick it back on the bike somehow and get your ass back on the road!" She's right as usual. My mouth was running faster than my brain and I mumbled something about having repair stuff on the bike and I'll call her again later and I'm sorry for worrying her and I love her. Gotta go.

I had also called Bob Wooldridge and left a message to see if there was a dealership nearby where I could get parts if needed. Bob owns a motorcycle dealership in Georgia and had volunteered to coordinate helping riders who had machine breakdowns throughout the rally. His first exercise happened in the first hours of the first day of the rally when a rider's BMW suffered a clutch failure.

As I was working on the bike he called back, and I told him what had happened and he told me the same thing as Susie had done but with a bit more "color" in the conversation.

In my spare parts stores were bolts and oversized washers. It only took me twenty minutes to empty the saddlebag, reattach it to the BMW, and repack my gear. In the saddlebag I found a handful of gravel that had been scooped up through the hole in the bag as I rode merrily down the road. Lord only knows how long the bag had been loose from the motorcycle.

Just as I was swinging my leg over the bike to get moving, three Harley Davidson riders saw me on the side of the interstate and pulled off to offer help. They stopped one hundred feet west of me and I gave them a thumbs-up and a wave. I got three thumbs-up in return and we all pulled back onto the highway headed west.

At the next fuel stop I adjusted the side-stand angle so the BMW would lean farther over when on the stand, and hoped that this was the last of the calamities to befall me on this rally.

The reattached saddlebag

There were five more bonuses to go in the leg. It was Saturday, day six, and I was an hour or so behind my plan due to the saddlebag and the foot-peg problems. Worse yet is that I only got two of the planned four hours of sleep in Vicksburg, and I knew that I would pay for this as the day wore on. So I mounted up and headed for Tyler, Texas which is just east of Dallas.

*   *   *   *   *   *   *   *   *   *   *

Tyler Pipe   *222 points*
Anytime
Tyler, Texas
Take a photo of the Tyler Pipe sign.
Category: Industrial hazard.
A January 2003 New York Times story began, "It is said that only the desperate seek work at Tyler Pipe." Over the course of ten years more than 4,600 workers were injured at this

plant due to improperly contained and handled industrial wastes.

*   *   *   *   *   *   *   *   *   *   *

The Tyler bonus went smoothly; I checked on my saddlebag mounts and then turned for Weatherford, Texas just a few hours and 159 miles away for another low point bonus. Texas was hot, but dry, and traffic was manageable.

*   *   *   *   *   *   *   *   *   *   *

Uncle Joe's Pawn   *150 points*
Anytime
Weatherford, Texas
Take a photo of the front of Uncle Joe's Pawn.
Category: Bank robbery, violation of bail.

Three men were in jail in Fort Worth for sex crimes. Two made bail, then proceeded to rob banks in Saginaw and Blue Mound to raise bail money to spring their associate. The plan succeeded briefly until they were spotted leaving this pawn shop.

*   *   *   *   *   *   *   *   *   *   *

This bonus required riding in heavy weekend traffic through a moderate sized town in hot weather and I would much rather be making miles on the highway than puttering through a town. It seemed as if everyone and their brother were out on the road. Next up was a quick 270 mile excursion to Lubbock for 407 points and then there were only two more bonuses before the checkpoint.

*   *   *   *   *   *   *   *   *   *   *

United Spirit Arena   *407 points*
Anytime
Lubbock, Texas
Take a photo of the stone marker indicating "United Spirit Arena."
Category: Abuse of sports officials.
Quarrelsome, abusive, and dictatorial Bobby Knight retired as head coach here at Texas Tech in February 2008, causing basketball referees throughout the land to emit a collective sigh of relief.
*   *   *   *   *   *   *   *   *   *   *

The parking area at this bonus was similar to a roach motel. You can check in but you can't check out. I spent five minutes trying to get back to the main road, which was just a few feet away across a grass island. The traffic arrows kept trying to point me toward the rear of the arena so I finally just rode across the grass and headed west.

At this point I figured that I was back on plan with 162 miles to go to Billy the Kid's grave, which would be the last bonus of the day, and I could stop for rest somewhere west of the bonus. I left Lubbock at 5:20 p.m. and planned on getting to the grave just before sundown with a bit of time to spare.

After calling Susie for the third time to apologize for my dumb-ass phone call that morning, I settled in for a few hours of quiet riding. It didn't last.

About eighty miles out from Fort Sumner and the grave-site the afternoon thundershowers started to develop around me. US Highway 60 is a good road but it's not a fast road, as there are a lot of small towns to pass through and in most of these the speed limit drops to twenty-five or so.

Every time I saw the reduce speed signage I dropped down to a crawl and that really was killing my time, so this part of the ride took longer than I planned.

I still had time to make the grave-site but there was no longer any time to spare. In fact it looked like I would be biting into the one-hour-after-sunset timing that the rules allow.

When getting a daylight-only photo bonus the rider is supposed to show that they were at the bonus during a period that starts an hour before sunrise and ends an hour after sunset. This is usually easy to do by showing that distant objects can be seen in the light. If distant objects can't be seen, the rider has to obtain a computer generated receipt from a nearby business to demonstrate that they were within the daylight window.

Twenty miles from the bonus I was riding along and pacing a long, fast-moving freight train to my left (south). The engineer and I had exchanged waves and blown our horns at each other (his were louder). This was fun riding. Then I looked at the GPS and noticed that the bonus was off of the main highway and to the south as well. Crap, another thing to worry about.

I was not going to race the train, but if it got to the side road before I did I would not have time to make the bonus before the train cleared the entrance road. On top of that, the storms were now all around the bonus, lightening was searing to the ground, it was raining, and it was getting dark.

I was near the bonus, pacing a train at the speed limit, in the rain, near sunset, and I needed all of the points I could get. All this is whirling around in my mind like a dervish. At least the saddlebags and foot-pegs are still attached.

This was why I was riding in the IBR. I wasn't frustrated by the fact that the train may cost me the bonus. I was actually laughing at the karma that had drawn me, the train, the thundershowers, the bonus, and the IBR together all at the same time.

Five miles from the bonus the rain let up, I zoomed in the view on the GPS to get more detail of the location, and low-and-behold the train tracks appeared on the screen and they veered off to the south just before the entrance to the grave-site. The train and the rain were out of the equation. Now it was just about getting there and proving that I was there within the time window.

*   *   *   *   *   *   *   *   *   *   *

Billy the Kid's grave   *872 points*
Daylight hours only
Old Fort Sumner, New Mexico
*Take a photo of the headstone of Billy the Kid's grave. There is a replica grave at the Billy the Kid Museum. That is **not** an acceptable substitute. The actual cemetery is located on the grounds of the Fort Sumner State Monument.*
Category: Banditry.
This is the final resting place of William (Billy the Kid) Bonney and two of his associates. The grave stone has been stolen repeatedly over the years, so this one is made with reinforced concrete. Billy was gunned down near here by Sheriff Pat Garrett on the night of 7/14/1881. His last words, in Spanish, were, "¿Quién es? (Who is it?). Garrett himself was shot and killed outside of Las Cruces, New Mexico on 2/29/1908. We don't know what his last words were.
*   *   *   *   *   *   *   *   *   *   *

I did wander around in the parking lot for a few minutes in the twilight trying to find the grave-site. There was a small building, but no signs directing patrons to the grave. I finally found it behind the museum building. It was in a small courtyard surrounded by a wrought-iron fence to prevent folks from stealing the headstone.

I took my photos but I needed to use the flash to get the flag to show clearly, as it was getting dark fast. I then planted the camera solidly on a fencepost and took some long exposures of the sky, which had a streak of horizontal light across it, to try and prove that I was there on time. But the photos were still not definitive in terms of daylight, so I headed into Fort Sumner, New Mexico, for a receipt as the clock was ticking down.

The skyline showing a small amount of daylight.

On the way out of the side road I passed a rider who was heading toward the bonus and realized that I was not alone in this craziness and some other rider was even later than I. The other rider was Matt Watkins and we met up at the convenience store in town a few miles away. I entered the store, grabbed the first soft drink I saw, and handed my credit card to the cashier to get a receipt. I made the deadline with a few minutes to spare. Matt was right on the money. Way too close for comfort.

It has always amazed me that 101 riders moving about the country on different routes can run into one another fairly regularly. Matt and I talked for a short while about the R60 and how well it was doing and how his ride was going thus far. He was doing well and his Yamaha FJR was running flawlessly.

However, he had lost his keys somewhere between parking his motorcycle at the gas pumps and the store, a distance of fifty feet. I offered to help look for them but he thought that they were somewhere in his saddlebag and said that he would use his spare set. We were both tired and heading west but not in the same westerly direction. I wished him well and we headed our separate ways.

My plan called for a visit to one more bonus in Prescott, Arizona, and then on to Santa Ana, California, which is the checkpoint. There were several other bonuses I could add on the way if I felt up to it, so I headed west and planned to stop for sleep around Gallup, New Mexico. It was 575 miles, or about nine hours, to Prescott and then 463 miles and another seven hours to Santa Ana. I again decided to get into the checkpoint for early scoring so I could check out the BMW and get as much sleep as possible before starting the third and last leg.

Bonus points are always higher on the last leg. A bonus that may have been worth a paltry 100 points for a certain distance and difficulty on the first leg may be worth twenty times that amount on the last leg, and I figured that I was still over the point value needed to "finish". That was including the two call-in bonuses and the rest bonus.

As I rode west the temperature dropped into the high 40s and I stopped to get my cool weather gear on. I am limited in terms of space on the bike and can carry just so much clothing. For temperatures from 50F into the hundred-plus range I make do with LD Comfort brand underwear and my riding suit. When the air gets colder I add a pair of fleece pants and an electrically heated jacket. This keeps me good into the 20s.

The fleece pants speak for themselves. They are warm and made for a motorcycle rider. The heated jacket is made like a windbreaker so that there is no bulk and it can be worn into the 70s. It is fitted with resistance wires similar to an electric blanket and can put out eighty-five watts of heat to my chest, back, neck, and arms. I have an electric controller built into the left hand-grip on the BMW that lets me change the heat setting on the jacket as I ride so I can stay comfortable and the setup works extraordinarily well.

I had one other run-in with rally riders during the night. I stopped for fuel in the middle of nowhere at a combination gas station/casino. I don't even remember what state I was in. After I filled the tanks I grabbed a cup of coffee and a snack in the station and walked back to the pump. I was standing next to my bike relaxing for a few seconds and out of the empty night a clear voice says "I see that antique is still running." It was Tom and Rosie Sperry on the other side of the pump island and the comment made me grin. Tom and Rosie were riding the IBR two-up on a Honda Gold Wing. They were fine and headed to California.

I had stopped prior to this refueling for three hours of sleep in a motel but shortly after riding away from Tom and Rosie I started to get weary. Over years of long-distance riding I had learned to recognize when I am truly getting sleepy. I also understand that any other goal is secondary to the safe completion of the ride.

Usually I stop for a nap when I yawn widely for the third time. Another indicator is when I notice that I have had a nonsense thought. That is, some incongruous thought that makes no sense under the circumstances. A final sign that I need to consider stopping is when I realize that I have to concentrate on holding a steady speed.

When any of these things happens I pull off of the road and nap. Knowing when to stop and rest is the hallmark of a successful long-distance rider. In this case I found the next truck stop, put the bike under a streetlight in a corner of the lot, and checked into the Iron Butt Motel for a half-hour.

I simply lay down on the asphalt next to the BMW, with my helmet still on, and closed my eyes. This is the only time on this IBR that I slept in the Iron Butt Motel. I decided right then and there that I was going to increase my motel stops to a full four hours so I wouldn't have to do it again.

-Day Seven, Sunday-

The next morning I found six riders at the bonus in Prescott at 11:00 a.m. Even though we all waved at each other I could see that everyone, including me, was concentrating on the last push to Santa Ana.

* * * * * * * * * * *

Hastings Books Music & Video   *2,211 points*
Anytime
Prescott, Arizona
Take a photo of the exterior of the building identifying it as Hastings.
Category: Theft, credit card appropriation.
A thief stole a woman's purse. Later the criminal and victim found themselves together by accident in this bookstore, she to complain about $200 charges on her credit card and he to buy some more DVDs with her card.
* * * * * * * * * * *

Prescott was a busy, crowded city with lots of traffic, but the temperature was in the low eighties and not a cloud in the sky, and this is the kind of riding I love. After securing the bonus I headed out of town on highway 89 which was another road on this rally that reminded me a lot of the Blue Ridge Parkway back home. Twisty, curvy, somewhat green, cool, good road surface, and a joy to ride. I should add that it was a joy to ride safely at the speed limit because I waved as I passed by each of the officers in four patrol cars using laser speed detectors spaced every mile from the city limits.

Highway 89 descended through hill-country into flatland in a fairly quick amount of time and I suddenly realized I was riding across one of those areas where I wonder why anyone would bother to build a road. The land was mostly flat and featureless with sparse, low dry scrub growing along the highway. There were local roads every now and then which meant that someone lived in what appeared to be a large, dry, hot, wasteland. Why?

On local highway 71 the temperature rose to over 100 degrees; the heat was palpable and the desert got dryer. Now, anyone who tells you that the heat in the desert Southwest is a "dry" heat is correct. But when they invariably add that this makes it tolerable they are absolutely wrong. My thermometer hit 113 before noon and it was definitely not "tolerable". It was brutal.

As I rode I remembered one of the reasons for my DNF in 2007 was dehydration and I was making sure that I was sucking down water. I carried a gallon water jug which I filled at each stop. I made it a point to drink a few long pulls on the bite-valve every ten minutes whether I felt like drinking or not.

At the next stop I followed the advice I'd been given by quite a few long-distance riders and sealed up my riding suit. Yes, it's counter-intuitive to close all the openings on my clothing in the desert heat, but it worked very well. I zipped up the jacket and closed all of the vents in the jacket and pants except for a small one on my back. I even closed the sleeve vents and my helmet visor and this made the ride considerably more bearable. Not pleasant by any means, but tolerable.

Whenever I ride the motorcycle I rely on specially made underwear that is manufactured and distributed by a long-distance rider who got tired of not being able to find comfortable gear for the type of riding that we do. The material is made to wick moisture away from the skin so my skin stays dry and the evaporation keeps me cool. I was wearing a black long-sleeved turtle neck top and shorts. During cold weather the fact that I was dry helped keep me comfortable and during hot weather the wicking action helped keep me cool.

I had learned many years before, that riding without a jacket or long pants in the desert created more problems than it solved. Shorts and a T-shirt allow the sun to bake the rider's arms and legs. They also allow a lot of moisture to evaporate quickly. This doesn't actually cool the rider but it does use up a lot of the rider's water and can quickly lead to dehydration.

When folks comment that I must be deranged to ride in full protective gear in the summer heat I usually remark that they may want to think of photographs they've seen of nomads in the desert. They are not wearing tank tops and shorts. They wear long sleeved robes that reach the ground. The covering protects them from the sun and slows down the evaporation of moisture from the skin.

By 1:00 p.m. the temperature had risen to 116 and stayed there for most of the next two hundred miles. This was the highest temperature I'd ever ridden in. I played with opening the face shield on the helmet to see if the moving air would cool me down at speed and it was as if someone was holding a hairdryer on *high* a few inches from my face. Shield down was the way to go.

Just a few miles before my last planned fuel stop prior to the checkpoint I got a phone call from Bill Thweatt. First thing he said was, "Are you using the ice trick?" I'd completely forgotten about the ice trick. Bill had found in a previous IBR that putting a bag of ice down the front of your riding jacket so it sits on the crotch makes a big difference in surviving this king of relentless, skull-baking heat. Also, if the rider places the bag correctly they can enjoy popping frosty ice cubes in their mouth as they ride.

Bill was on his third bag today and was about a hundred miles away. At the next small oasis I pulled in for my two burger snack and fuel. The burgers were $2.50 each instead of the usual ninety-nine cents. I guess you can charge what you want when you are the only service within fifty miles.

On the other hand a bag of ice was just half a buck. I filled the fuel tanks and then provided entertainment for the folks at the pumps as I placed two bags of ice down the inside of my jacket and then shifted around to move the ice a bit farther down if you follow my drift. I can tell you that the trick worked. It made the difference between a really nasty experience and an endurable ride. It was also outlandish to be sucking on ice cubes while riding in the middle of the fiercely-dry and blistering desert.

I'm thankful to Bill, not just for reminding me about the "ice-trick", but for the three or four phone conversations we had every day of the rally. I enjoyed hearing from another rider who was going through the same sort of twisted fun that I was. We were keeping check on each other's sanity and experiences as well as just passing the time. Bill also enjoyed the phone calls, except for the one time he broke off in the middle of a sentence to say "Damn, I just missed the exit for my bonus."

About forty miles out from Santa Ana I started to smell smoke from forest fires that were burning in the Los Angeles area. As I got closer I could see a huge loom-up of smoke on the horizon, and in the last few miles I was able to make out what appeared to be an entire mountain range on fire to the east of the city. From some angles the smoke column resembled that from an atomic bomb. I've been a fireman for thirty years and I have worked some large brush fires, but a large brush fire in my neck of the woods is ten or fifteen acres.

I wouldn't know where to begin fighting a fire the size of the one I was staring at.

As I approached the checkpoint I was feeling good, had stories to tell about losing the saddlebag, breaking the foot-peg, surviving the desert, pacing the train, and actually I had really had a good time. In fact, other than the two mishaps, I had been feeling cheerful about the ride from the very start.

I pulled into the checkpoint at 4:12 p.m., a few hours before early scoring and five hours prior to the official opening time of 9:00 p.m. As I arrived at the parking lot someone walked up to me and asked to see my "maximum speed" on my GPS. He looked official with a clipboard in his hand but he did not have an IBR identification card around his neck so I figured he was a troublemaker. Most GPSs will display the maximum speed reached and most of the time the speed shown is highly inaccurate due to problems with satellite reception.

For example, every time that I would travel Interstate 95 between North Carolina and New Jersey I would pass through the Baltimore Harbor Tunnel and my GPS would lose the satellite for a minute or two. When I exited the tunnel it recomputed the distance it thought I had traveled in a very short period of time and displays a top speed in the two hundred mile per hour range. This is highly entertaining, but seriously misleading.

I didn't know why this person wanted to see the maximum speed but I had already looked at it on the way into Santa Ana and it read 327.4 miles per hour. I showed it to him and he looked at the GPS, then at the R60, then at me, and again at the GPS. He muttered something about needing to reset it to zero and wandered away. I just smiled.

I parked the BMW and checked in with Ira Agins to stop my clock for the leg. I went to my room to get my paperwork and photos in order. My plan was to get through scoring, retrieve a "care-package" that I had previously sent to Santa Ana that contained a change in underwear and three quarts of motor oil, check the valves on the BMW, and then get some sleep.

There is usually a lot of activity at checkpoints. The riders catch up on maintenance, change worn tires, repair equipment that has broken, and make sure that their motorcycle is ready for the next leg. In the 2007 rally I had changed my rear tire at the checkpoint. This rally I was going to ride throughout the event on the same tires, but I had sent a new rear tire to the finish checkpoint in Spokane in case I needed it for the ride back to North Carolina.

I've noticed through the years that there is a big difference between how I mentally picture myself and how I actually appear to others. I still feel inside just as I did when I was in college in the early 1970s, but every time I look in a mirror I wonder who the old man is. As I sat down at the scoring table with Greg Roberts he took my picture. I felt as if I was in great shape, alert, slightly tired, but still sharp. The picture shows a slightly different view.

At scoring I did well with one exception, and a big one at that. Remember my comments about reading comprehension? I had misread the time for the first call-in bonus. I thought that both bonuses were noon to midnight

Pacific Time. There is no good reason for me to have thought that as the listing for the first bonus clearly says midnight to noon Pacific Time. Eight riders had failed to call in, and sixteen, including me, had called in late. There went four hundred and ninety-nine very easy points.

* *

Call-In Bonus - no specific location   499 points   Available August 28, 2009
12:01 am to noon Pacific time
Call xxx xxx-xxxx and leave the following information:
* *

I ended the leg with 35,550 points in 75th place and about four hundred and fifty-five points below what was needed to officially "finish" for the leg. I had traveled 3,678 miles in eighty-four hours with an average overall speed of forty-three miles per hour. Not bad for a thirty-three year old motorcycle with 517,000 miles on it (or a fifty-six year old rider).

The R60 did well throughout the leg. The bike handled well and wasn't bothered by the desert heat or the nineteen hours a day of riding. At the checkpoint I did have several folks wander up to take pictures of the foot-peg and the saddlebag. When I was kneeling on the asphalt checking on the valve clearances, several more offered to help if the BMW was broken. I explained that it was just a valve check and everything was alright. I appreciated the offers of help, but the R60 was doing just fine.

8 Leg Three - Santa Ana to Spokane

-Day Eight, Monday-

Monday August 31st started just like the first day of the last leg. I was awake at 3:30 a.m. and had set up the maps and equipment I needed to plan a route. The bike was uncovered and ready as we were gathering for the 4:00 a.m. distribution of the bonus listing. I knew that I was four hundred and fifty points under the "finisher" total but I also knew that this leg was ninety-nine hours, roughly four days, and that the points-per-bonus would be higher than the last two legs.

The riders were starting to show the wear and tear of the last seven days. There was not as much talking or joshing as there was in Spartanburg or St. Charles. There was also less nervousness about the upcoming leg. Those riders hoping for a podium finish were finding out who was in what place and knew that this was the deciding leg of the rally. Those hoping to earn finisher status were adding up the points they had and gearing up to meet the minimum for the final leg that Tom Austin would shortly announce.

Mike Kneebone announced the names of the top ten riders.

Position	Rider	Points
First	Jeff Earls	62438
Second	Jim Owen	61667
Third	Eric Jewell	59951
Fourth	Andy Mills	54645
Fifth	Roger Sinclair	54096
Sixth	Matt Watkins	53830
Seventh	Chris Sakala	53472
Eighth	Ken Meese	52444
Ninth	Michael Evans	52209
Tenth	Bob Lilly	50883

Jeff Earls, Jim Owen, and Eric Jewell were in the top three slots. All three of these riders are quiet, easy-going, and unassuming. They have always been easy to talk to and more than willing to share their experience. To look at any of them you wouldn't think that they are the foremost long-distance endurance motorcycle riders in the world. Their ability to figure out the puzzle of a rally, manage the energy and fatigue required to ride, and the relentless inner strength to complete the ride at the top of the standings time after time is staggering.

After the bonus packs were handed out I spent a little over three hours developing a route for this third, and last, leg. This is a nerve-racking part of the rally. It took time to read all of the bonus information, and more time to find the bonus locations on my map. While I was running different routes through my mapping software, I was subconsciously fretting that I was spending way too much time working out my route.

I worried that I would be the last rider to hit the road toward the finish. I agonized that I would miss another critical bonus as I'd done with the house of ill-repute in leg two. I worried that I was worrying. When I realized this last bit, it dawned on me that I was wasting energy that I would need to finish the rally. I got my act back on track, and worked out my route. When I was happy with the timing and the distances involved I checked in with Susie to tell her I was heading out, and feeling good.

Leaving Santa Ana on the last leg (Photo by Steve Hobart)

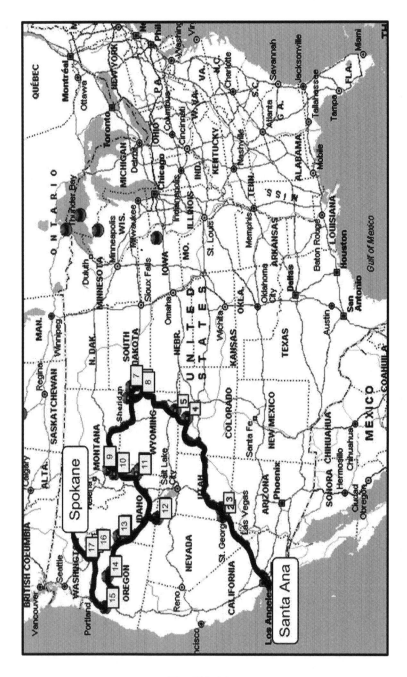

The third leg

I left Santa Ana at 7:15, and half of the motorcycles were still in the parking lot. I was bound for the Mountain Meadows Memorial in Utah, four hundred miles and six hours away. As I made the first shift into gear on the R60 I again felt the discomfort of the dislodged toe liner of my left boot pressing on my big toe. Every single morning it bothered me, but after an hour or so I no longer noticed it.

I planned on getting a bonus in Rand, Colorado, first thing Tuesday morning followed by a trip northeast to large bonuses at Crazy Horse Mountain in South Dakota and Devils Tower in Wyoming.

After that I would ride through Montana, Nevada, and Idaho for a few average-point bonuses, and on the last day of the rally I would get a large bonus near Antelope, Oregon, and then work my way toward the finish, picking up a few more bonuses in Oregon and Washington.

I hoped for four hours of sleep Tuesday and Wednesday and then planned to ride straight through the final twenty-four hours until the finish.

My start was inauspicious because as I left Santa Ana I missed my ramp to I-15 and spent five minutes circling through the freeway system while the helpful voice of my GPS was yelling at me through my helmet speakers that I was "Off-course" and asking if it should "Recalculate" over and over and over and over again. Madness was near. A few minutes later I was finally back on track and eastbound.

In rides prior to this IBR I did not have my phone connected to my communications system and I would have to pull off of the road to make or receive calls. However, that takes time from riding and there were times that my wife couldn't reach me. For this rally I had added a hookup to my CB radio so that I could receive and make phone calls hands-free. This turned out to be a boon because Susie and I talked three or four times a day.

The only person I talked with on a daily basis was Bill Thweatt as we kept track of each other's progress. Bill helped me stay alert and entertained and I hope that I did the same for him. It truly helped to talk with someone who was going through the same things that I was.

However, in this day and age of instant communication it is hard for people to fall off of the net as I tried to do during the rally. Just because I was on vacation didn't mean that folks from work would stop calling. Most of these were easy to handle diversions, like the time the gatehouse at one of my plants in North Carolina called to ask if a delivery man could enter the property. It was easier to give permission to the guard than to explain that I was three thousand miles away in the middle of a desert.

As I was leaving the Los Angeles area at the start of this leg I got a call from someone at work. My phone doesn't ring when a call is received so the first I would know of an incoming call was when the person at the other end would hear the wind noise from my motorcycle and say something like "Hello----hello".

I heard the "Hello" and answered. I explained that I was on vacation and the caller insisted that I had to deal with an order that I had placed before I left. I mentioned that I was on the motorcycle and he persisted that it would only take a few minutes to sort out. I brought up that I was riding in Los Angeles Monday morning rush hour traffic and he asked the questions he had for me anyway. I answered everything that he asked and he told me to hang on for a minute while he checked some paperwork. As he shuffled through his papers I got his attention and combined all of the information I had tried to get through to him before. I was on vacation, on the bike, riding in the IBR, in rush hour L.A. traffic, and was signing off.

Just before the California border I stopped for fuel. Riding in the 2007 Iron Butt Rally taught me that I could ride more efficiently if I created various routines to follow. I had a set routine for getting gas, for planning a route, for a check of the R60 before I started out each day, for documenting a bonus, for sleeping, and for eating.

My routine for a typical fuel stop began by finding a modern station with pay-at-the-pump so I wouldn't have to waste time going into the station to pay and get a receipt. I put the credit card into the pump and while the card was processing I opened both fuel tanks and then I would start fueling. After I replaced the gas-pump hose I waited to see if I had to enter a request for a receipt as I closed the main tank and put the tank bag back in place. I got the receipt from the pump and placed a check mark next to the city, state, time, and gallons to be sure that the information was correct, because all of the information had to be present or a rider would lose points. Then I wrote the odometer reading and the real time on the receipt and placed the receipt in my document bag.

There are stories galore about riders who lost their receipts during the rally. One rider, Sean Gallagher, lost his receipt bag while riding from Key West to the Denver checkpoint in 2005. He spent long hours looking for the bag and even offered a reward for it, but in the end he lost all points associated with the bonus and his fuel log for the leg. After Gallagher told me about losing his receipts and the time and angst that it caused him, I decided not to let this happen to me. My receipts went into a waterproof zippered bag that was attached to my riding suit by a one foot cord and stored in a zippered pocket that held nothing else.

There was no pay-at-the-pump at the first station I pulled into. With the clock ticking I entered the station and was told that California does not have pay-at-the-pump (the clerk lied) and I would have to put down a fifty dollar deposit before I could fuel. This was eating into my time, but I could just see the sign for another gas station across the Interstate and decided to head there. Low-and-behold there was a new gas station equipped with modern pay-at-the-pump dispensers, and they charged less for gas as well.

A short while later as I approached Las Vegas, Nevada, I looked down to check my route sheet in the clear top of my tank bag and the sheet was gone. The route sheet is a three by five inch card that is an abbreviated description of where I need to travel during the leg. Since this is how I keep track of my bonuses and routing I decided to stop for gas and food while I pulled out my laptop to recopy my route sheet. This was not the way to start the last leg of the IBR.

```
MMM  4835 d   3p
COC  169 d    3:45
     -4 hours -
COP 4568 d    6 Am
LRm  267      7:30 A
OTw 5837 2    1:15 p  Tues
CHm 4920
     - 7 hrs -
ToR  288 d    9:30 A wed
BSk 1818 d    1:30 p
JkP 2370      8p
     - Rest Bonus -
```

```
BAG 3874 d   11 Am. Thurs
Cvs 3576     3p.
PSD 1070     8p Thurs
Red Low      10.47pm
```

Pictured above are the front and back of the route sheet I used on the third leg. It told me the IBR code for the bonus, the point value, whether it is a daylight only bonus ("d"), and the time I should be at the bonus. With the bike and myself full and the routing card once again properly in place it was just a few more hours to the first bonus of the leg.

* * * * * * * * * * *

Mountain Meadows memorial   *4,835 points*
Daylight hours only
Enterprise and Veyo, Utah
Take a photo of the memorial cairn. The parking lot is about one mile from the main highway on a dirt road. The road may be closed during rain. If so, take a photo of the memorial that overlooks the valley to the west. It is a short walk from the parking lot nearest the highway.
Category: Mass murder.
In September 1857 the Fancher party emigrant train from Arkansas was attacked by Mormons at this site. On September 11, after a five-day battle, the assailants approached the embattled pioneers under a truce flag. They convinced the emigrants to surrender peacefully and to be led out of the valley under guard. On a prearranged signal, however, the Mormon militia shot and killed 120 men and women, leaving only 17 small children to survive. It remained

the worst mass murder in the country's history for exactly 144 years until the terrorist attacks of 9/11/2001.

* * * * * * * * * * *

It was unsettling to read the bonus description. Beyond the wretched fact that the mass murder occurred, was it coincidence or something greater that it happened 144 years to the day before 9/11?

There were several riders at the memorial. I took a short hike to the bonus, took my picture, and filled out the bonus sheet. Then I was off to Cedar City, Utah, for a 152 point bonus just an hour, sixty miles, away.

As I left Mountain Meadows I noticed that there were forest fires burning near the bonus and the smoke from the fires seemed to concentrate in the canyons I was riding through. The air was tinged brown, and I could see the smoke and smell it for the next one hundred and twenty-five miles.

*   *   *   *   *   *   *   *   *   *   *

Church of Christ   *152 points*
Daylight hours only
Cedar City, Utah
Take a photo of the front of the church.
Category: Disorderly conduct.
Church of Christ minister Alfred Pehl was fined $321 for attempting to stop speeders in his neighborhood by blocking the road and threatening the motorists with shovels and broomsticks.

*   *   *   *   *   *   *   *   *   *   *

This was a quick, simple bonus on the way to a very large bonus in Rand, Colorado. The temperatures were in the mid to high nineties, but after the ride through the desert yesterday this was pleasant. I expected to be in Rand at daybreak Tuesday and would stop somewhere in Colorado for sleep during the 600 mile, ten hour ride.

Riding through the western US is breathtaking. Between the deserts, mountains, alpine forests, curvy roads, and even the dead-straight Interstates, I am always entertained by the geology. I especially liked to ride through Colorado, but on this IBR most of that particular ride was at night. In the darkness I couldn't see the scenery and I couldn't see the deer, hereafter referred to as "forest-rats", except when their beady little eyes lit up or when I saw the flash of a dirty brown hide streak across the road.

Bambi is not the cute little forest creature most people envision when it is standing by the side of the road and I don't know if it will stay in place, dart to the right, to the left, directly at me, or wherever else its peanut sized mind may decide to send it. Some riders fear drunk drivers, others fear folks on cell phones. I fear the wildlife.

A number of riders put deer-whistles on their motorcycles to warn the beasts that they are coming even though there is not a shred of scientific data to indicate that the whistles work. One year in my area of North Carolina there were several deer-strikes involving emergency vehicles responding to fires or rescues. I figure that if a deer does not shy away from a fifty thousand pound truck that is running an old fashioned wind-up siren, air horns, and has flashing white, red, and yellow lights, it will not react to a small whistle.

IBR riders have run into deer, antelope, moose, cattle, buffalo, coyotes, elk, bear, and countless other animals. In some cases the rider continues on with the ride; in other cases the injuries to rider and/or motorcycle end their rally. Hitting critters is one of the major hazards of riding a motorcycle, whether riding in the Iron Butt Rally, or just around one's neighborhood.

Other than watching for forest-rats only one other item of note happened this evening. My low beam headlight stopped working around 11:00. Unlike a typical headlight bulb, the high-intensity-discharge (HID) lighting on the R60 is made up of a bulb assembly and high-voltage ballast.

The latter is an electronic package that supplies a few thousand volts for a very short amount of time to start the bulb each time it is turned on. Not being able to light the road would be a big problem in deer country; however, this was a failure that I was prepared for, as I carried spare bulbs and had a spare ballast unit installed in the fairing. It took less than two minutes to swap bulbs and get back on the road.

-Day Nine, Tuesday-

After a stop for four hours in Grand Junction, Colorado, for some sleep I continued to Rand which was in the middle of absolutely nowhere. Since a lot of these bonuses are so far off of the beaten-path that there really is no path at all, I spent time wondering how the IBR organizers found them in the first place. I mean, who in the world visited Rand, Colorado, to find this bonus? Bob Higdon did.

Just before dawn as I was riding on Colorado Highway 14 approaching Highway 125 which would take me to Rand, my GPS told me to turn East off of the paved road and onto a gravel farm road to save a few miles. This happened three times, and three times I resisted. All of the side-roads were unnamed dirt farm roads that led into the blackness of the Colorado night. I just didn't want to take the chance that I would end up stranded in the middle of a pasture on a bad dirt road in the dark.

I stayed on the main roads, and as I approached the bonus, which was twenty miles west of Rocky Mountain National Park, the sun was just rising, and several riders passed by me on their way out of Rand. This let me know that I was on the right path to the bonus. It also meant that I was running behind several other riders.

*   *   *   *   *   *   *   *   *   *   *

Police car   *4,568 points*
Daylight hours only
Rand, Colorado
Take a photo of the police car and its occupant. It is parked next to the Rand Yacht Club on CO-125 on the east side of the highway.
Category: Crime fighter.
This town has found a unique way to maintain a constant vigil by its small but dedicated police force.
*   *   *   *   *   *   *   *   *   *   *

The police car was parked perpendicular to the only road in town and had a dummy behind the wheel. Stranger than that were the motorcyclists pulling over to place flags on the car and take a picture.

Not only was this bonus entertaining, but the mannequin and car were parked in front of the Rand Yacht Club and I was at 9,000 feet in the Colorado Mountains nowhere near a body of water.

The next bonus was in Laramie, Wyoming, just eighty-seven miles north.

* * * * * * * * * * *

JJ's Bar   *267 points*
Anytime
Laramie, Wyoming
Take a photo of the exterior of the building.
Category: Hate crime
Matthew Shepard, a gay student at the University of Wyoming, met two men at this bar, then known as the Fireside Lounge, on the night of 10/7/1998. They subsequently robbed, pistol whipped, and tortured him, leaving him tied to a fence in the

mountains to the east of town. He was found comatose 18
hours later and died a few days later. The killers are serving
life sentences.
*   *   *   *   *   *   *   *   *   *   *

Bob Higdon did a lot of work to come up with the
theme and bonuses for this rally and they are bouncing me
around not only from state to state but emotionally as well. In
the last twenty-four hours I visited the site of the largest
mass-murder short of 9/11, a place where street-justice
became laughable, the police car in Rand, and now the site of
a hate crime. I stopped across the street from the bar
because I just didn't feel right pulling up to the door and
taking a photograph of the place where a tragedy began.

After documenting the bonus it was time to head
northwest. Devil's Tower, Wyoming, was one of a cluster of
three bonuses in Wyoming and South Dakota that I needed to
get in order to have enough points to do well on the leg.
There was a clock counting down on this particular bonus
because I needed to take a picture in the Visitor's Center,

which closed at 7:00 p.m. The other large bonus was Crazy Horse Mountain and it was available daylight hours only.

The most efficient route to this cluster was to ride in an eastward arc to hit Crazy Horse, then northeast to the Deadwood Saloon in South Dakota, and finally west to Devil's Tower in Wyoming. Then I could continue west into Montana. However, because of road construction on the way to Devil's Tower, and the 7:00 deadline, I decided to ride to it first, and then circle east to Deadwood and south to Crazy Horse Mountain. This meant I would be retracing part of my route when I headed to Montana and that thought worried away at me as I rode.

If I was riding a modern motorcycle there was a very good chance that I would make better time through the twisty back roads and could cover the more efficient route. But while I love riding the R60, this option was just not open. Limited by fifty horsepower and the 1976 suspension, I had to work harder to cover miles than a rider on a newer cycle.

While I was working on my route in Santa Ana I had noticed warnings on my Streets & Trips mapping program that there was major road construction on the route I was planning to Wyoming, and when I hit the first of the construction projects it was a bear. Three long stretches where I had to wait fifteen minutes or more in the 100 degree sun for pilot cars. Then I would travel twenty miles or so and then repeat it again. There was entertainment though.

While waiting for the pilot cars I was passed by other rally riders who would ride to the head of the line of traffic and then take off right behind the pilot car. When we were back on the open road they would disappear into the distance but I would catch up with them at the next construction holdup.

Even with the road construction I made it to Devil's Tower by 2:30. I parked the BMW and glanced at the rock formation for a second as I headed into the visitor's center.

* * * * * * * * * * *

Visitor's Center   *5,837 points*
8:00 am. – 7:00 p.m.
Devil's Tower, Wyoming

Take a photo of the painting that hangs above the fireplace in the visitor's center. **Note:** Your ID flag does NOT have to be in this photo.

Category: Cross-breed adultery, bear baiting.

Although at least 20 tribes of Indians have treated this spectacular site as a sacred place, few of their legends describe clearly why they have wound up antagonizing the bear in such a fashion as the painting suggests. The Cheyenne story, however, is specific. It refers to the discovery by one brave that his wife, who had been hiding some deep scratches on her back, was actually having an affair with a very large bear. If true, that could easily account for the ill will between the species.

*   *   *   *   *   *   *   *   *   *   *

The small note you can barely see under the picture of the bear says "Do Not Use Flash In Building". I noticed it only after I had taken the flash photo.

Yet another part of my IBR experience was being at some truly remarkable location, in this case Devil's Tower, and not having the time to soak up the scene because the clock was ticking. The tower was monumental; it was huge and precise at the same time and set in the middle of a pretty cool forest. There were only a few visitors in the parking lot and if it had been any other time than during the Iron Butt I would have settled in for a while to walk around the tower and just look at the surroundings. However, the rally clock was ticking and I had time to look up at the tower for a few seconds while I was getting my riding gear in order and then had to go.

I did stop a mile away and was able to look the Tower over but it wasn't for the scenic content - it was because my cell phone suddenly showed three bars and I did my call-in bonus, twice. I carefully checked the time in the bonus instructions and then followed a checklist I had written out. I gave all of the information that was required, in the order it was called for. I was making absolutely sure I did not repeat the mistake of the last leg and miss some easy points. I was upset about losing the points for the call-in bonus. They were 499 points just for making a phone call. On top of that, it was just about the exact number of points I needed to make the finisher status guideline for that leg.

Deadwood was only an hour and a half to the east, traffic was moderate as I was riding through a tourist area, and when I arrived I found another IBR rider, Chris Sakala, just pulling in to take his photos. We both noticed that the bonus directions were not clear about just what the organizers wanted as proof of a visit.

* * * * * * * * * * *

Old Style #10 Saloon   *218 points*
Anytime
Deadwood, South Dakota
Take a photo of the Old Style #10 Saloon.
Category: Assassination, bragging to death.

While playing cards in a saloon — tourist legend has it that this is the place, but it really isn't — on 8/2/1876 Bill Hickok was shot in the back of the head by Jack McCall. The killer was tried but acquitted in a territorial court. Later, after bragging about how he'd fooled the law, McCall was tried again for Hickok's murder (double jeopardy didn't apply, since South Dakota was not then part of the United States). The second time wasn't the charm for McCall: he was convicted and hanged.

*   *   *   *   *   *   *   *   *   *   *

There are two pictures here because there are two #10 saloons next to each other. The "Old" #10 is at the wrong street address and the "Saloon #10" is at the address spelled out in the bonus packet. The best solution was to take photos of both saloons and move on. This turned out to be perfectly acceptable to the scorer when I sat down at the finish in Spokane.

My plan next called for a visit to Crazy Horse Mountain which was just an hour south. Riding to the Crazy Horse bonus was refreshing. There was little traffic and the roads twisted and turned through dense forests and between low mountain ranges. We just don't have riding like this on the east coast, and the R60 was a joy to ride through the curves. The thirty-three year old bike was doing just fine.

The temperature was in the mid-eighties, which was a substantial change from that morning. This was just about the perfect setting for riding a motorcycle.

*   *   *   *   *   *   *   *   *   *   *

Crazy Horse Mountain   *4,980 points*
Anytime
Entrance, Avenue of the Chiefs
Crazy Horse Mountain, South Dakota
Take a photo of the large sign pointing the way to the entrance to Crazy Horse Mountain.
Category: Destruction of private property.

A vandal took a hammer to Korczak Ziolkowski's magnificent sculptures that used to line the entrance leading up to the visitor's center. In 1939 Ziolkowski worked as an assistant to Gutzon Borglum on the Mount Rushmore memorial before beginning this epic project in 1948. After the sculptor's death in 1982, the work continues on this memorial through his family. In their 60+ years of labor on this monument, the Ziolkowskis have never accepted a dime of government funding.

*   *   *   *   *   *   *   *   *   *   *

I snapped my photo, logged my bonus information, and decided it was time to take a look at the rest of the leg's routing. I sat in the dirt parking lot and set up my laptop in the shadow of the BMW and reviewed the route I would be riding over the next two days.

As I was concentrating on my route, I heard a voice remarking on how riders seem to run into one another during the rally, and I look up to see another IBR rider, Bob St. George. Bob and I got to talking and I noticed his bike, a Yamaha FJR, was missing a lot of the material on the right side. It turns out that the night before while I was dodging forest-rats in Colorado he had the misfortune of hitting one.

Bob wasn't hurt but the bike had lost a saddlebag, bits of plastic, and all of the lighting on the right side. He found and reattached the saddlebag and then duct taped the larger pieces of bodywork in a pile to the side of the bike. There were wires for turn signals and other lights that were just taped to the side of the front cowling. It was ugly. He said that by the time he had talked with law enforcement his battery had run down and he had to wait for a jump start before he could continue on the rally.

Now, most riders would be ready to give up and head for the barn after hitting a deer at night in a state far from home. Not St. George. He told me that he had been thinking of dropping out of the rally <u>before</u> he hit the deer but after he hit it he decided that he simply had to finish what he started. Bob is a short, wiry rider who personifies the idea of the World's Toughest Motorcycle Rally.

After Bob and I parted, I decided I was going to hang with my plan to make my next bonus, Bozeman, Montana, and I headed out toward I-90, which meant retracing a hundred miles of the same road I traveled this afternoon. But I had the points in hand from this cluster of bonuses and was bolstered quite a bit by Bob's tale.

I called Susie to let her know that when she saw a circle on the satellite tracking map it did not mean that I was once again confused and wandering aimlessly in the west as I had done in 2007, but that I had to do it because of the bonus locations. Hearing her voice always gave me a lift. She was my voice of reason and I could count on her to ask questions so she could see if I was copacetic or not.

Bozeman was a daylight only bonus and eight and a half hours west. I planned on stopping somewhere along the 524 mile route for the rest bonus and being at the photo bonus early on Wednesday.

*   *   *   *   *   *   *   *   *   *   *
Rest Bonus - *no specific location   6,003 points*
Must start on Wednesday, September 2, 2009.   Stop for 5 or
more hours.
*   *   *   *   *   *   *   *   *   *   *

A rest bonus is a gift from the organizers. They are giving the riders a large amount of points to sleep. All the rider has to do is start the bonus within the time-frame set by the staff, and document the stop.

I would stop at a motel with a gas station nearby to make sure I could get a room before getting gas and the receipt, which starts the rest bonus clock. Then it's back to the motel to get some sleep. At the end of the bonus I would revisit the same gas station and get another receipt proving I had stopped for the required amount of time.

During the 2007 IBR I stayed at motels for the rest bonuses but spent most of my other rest stops at the Iron Butt Motel. While I did this a lot during my regular long-distance rides, I found during the IBR that I was not getting enough quality sleep for an eleven day rally.

I can fall asleep on a picnic table or on the sidewalk. However, I do sleep lightly and every time that I would hear a noise I would wake up. I guess that is a good survival trait but it's lousy when it comes to getting several hours of needed sleep. I made up my mind that for the 2009 IBR I would spend the money to stay at motels every day for sleeping.

While this led to better, uninterrupted sleep, it did chew a bit into the rally clock. It also chapped me to spend $85.00 for a four hour stay. Motels and hotels make a lot of noise about their amenities. Cable TV, Wi-Fi, great bedding, sterilized TV remote controls, and continental breakfasts to name but a few. Usually all I wanted was to stumble into a quiet room and sleep for four hours. Once I didn't even get out of my riding suit before falling asleep. Every second in the room not spent sleeping was a second that I would regret the next day.

I had a bag on the bike that I would carry into the room. It had the chargers for my cell phone and laptop, my alarm clock, sticky notes, and pen. I would write myself a note on my location and wake-up time, plug in the chargers, and be asleep within five minutes.

This night, I grabbed a full, five hours of sleep. It may not sound like much, but I was thankful for every minute of it.

-Day Ten, Wednesday-

I arrived in Bozeman just after sunrise and just in time for the morning rush hour. It also seemed as if most of the school buses in the city were traveling along the same narrow, two lane road that I was. I would ride a thousand feet and then wait a minute or two while kids climbed aboard the buses. I repeated this time after time for almost an hour. All the while, the rally clock was ticking. This was even more painful to me than visiting the college campus in Mississippi.

The rally organizers knew that most of the riders would prefer to ride the wide open spaces, and grab bonuses that allow a quick entry and exit. There were bonuses like that in this rally, but the point values were generally lower than a bonus that offered difficult riding conditions, or required precise timing. The harder it was to obtain a bonus, the more it was worth.

*   *   *   *   *   *   *   *   *   *

Frontline Processing   *246 points*
Daylight hours only
Bozeman, Montana
Take a photo of the main entrance to the building.
Category: Receipt of obscene material.
Jeffrey Ziegler downloaded child pornography from his workplace computer in one of the businesses that operated in this building. He defended himself by claiming a right to privacy. The trial court disagreed, giving him a small fine and no jail time. He appealed, lost, and because of his persistence, the entire world now knows what his interests have been.
*   *   *   *   *   *   *   *   *   *

Back in the 70s I had two friends who lived in Bozeman and this gave me a handy excuse to visit the city every year. This also gave me the pretext for a month-long motorcycle trip through what I think is one of the most amazing parts of the world. Within a day's ride are Yellowstone National Park, Grand Teton National Park, and Glacier National Park, not to mention dozens of national forests and endless miles of scenic highway. In fact, if you get off of the Interstate Highway in Montana almost any road is a scenic road.

The Big Sky bonus was only an hour away and I traveled through the type of landscape that I would call perfect. Mountains and meadows are everywhere. There are pine forests, shallow but wide rivers, blue lakes surrounded by grassland and forest. The air in this part of the world is invigorating, the temperatures were in the upper seventies, and the sky is an absolute-blue that has to be seen to be understood.

It was the first time that I had been on these roads in three decades and I was thrilled to be riding in Montana again. It was the IBR and I was boogying along but I was soaking up the countryside as I went. I was a happy camper. Big Sky is aptly named and getting there was almost uneventful.

Almost. If you rely solely on a GPS for guidance you will eventually be led astray. The GPS will give instructions to turn on a nonexistent road, or an obviously incorrect road, or guide you on a roundabout path to your destination.

Back in the 2007 IBR I had this happen to me quite a few times, and as the rally wore on I realized that I had set my GPS to figure my route as if I was riding a "motorcycle". I was on a motorcycle, but this allowed it to pick narrow, winding roads for the route. I finally learned that if I used the GPS setting for a truck it would keep me on good, two lane roads, and a provide a more direct route to each bonus.

I had fewer of these episodes this rally than in 2007, but on the way to the Summit Hotel the GPS insisted I take a left on a two lane paved road, which turned into a one lane paved road, then gravel, and then I had to stop because I was just shy of a house right in the middle of what the GPS showed as a northbound road. I had actually traveled up a personal driveway.

I backtracked to the main road and turned left onto what was the real route to Big Sky even as the voice from the GPS insisted that I was "off-route" and was repeatedly asking if it should "recalculate". It's day ten of the rally and I knew that I was weary because I was arguing back with the voice. This time I won the argument.

* * * * * * * * * * *

Summit Hotel *1,818 points*
Daylight hours only
Big Sky Ski & Summer Resort
Take a photo of the Summit Hotel at Big Sky resort from the parking lot in front of the hotel.
Category: Abduction.
Kari Swenson, an Olympic biathlon star, was abducted by two mountain men in the woods not far from here on 7/15/1984. They thought she would make a fine wife for the younger kidnapper. Swenson was wounded and one man was killed in the course of her rescue.
* * * * * * * * * * *

I documented the bonus fairly quickly and headed back out to the main road. My plan called for me to go to Driggs, Idaho, and then Jackson, Wyoming, for two relatively small bonuses and then on to a casino for some larger points. Driggs and Jackson look fairly close together on the map and the plan was doable so I headed off on the 143 mile, three hour ride to find the home of MaryAnn from Gilligan's island.

As I rode farther and farther away from the big roads I realized that this was a blunder. Riding the miles and using the time to get these two small bonuses was too much for too little reward but I made that realization after I was committed to the first bonus. What made sense in Santa Ana didn't look as good on the road.

What did look good was the scenery. I had never ridden along the west side of the Teton Mountains and the views were spectacular.

I became interested in geology in the mid-seventies. I started paying attention to the land around me and found it fascinating to watch how different parts of North America were formed or are still being formed. For example, most folks are unaware that the Teton mountains, the range I was riding along, are growing an inch or so a year. The Rocky Mountains are also growing but more slowly. On the other hand the

Appalachian Mountains on the East Coast are what are left of the roots of a mountain range that millions of years ago were higher than Mt. Everest in the Himalayas is today.

If I had been doing anything but the IBR this would have been a great time, but I was fussing at myself for taking this side-trip and hustled on to Driggs where I found that the house that should now be a church was actually a brand new furniture store.

*   *   *   *   *   *   *   *   *   *   *

Idaho Film & Television Institute   *106 points*
Daylight hours only
Driggs, Idaho
Take a photo of the church that now occupies this address.
Category: Possession of marijuana.
Dawn Wells, who played Mary Ann on the sit-com Gilligan's Island and founded the Idaho Film & Television Institute, was arrested for possession of marijuana while driving home from a birthday party for her on 10/18/2007.
*   *   *   *   *   *   *   *   *   *   *

However, the street address was correct so I snapped the picture, noted the required information, and went into town to get a gas receipt to show that I was at the right location. I then headed back out to the big roads and a casino in Nevada. This would be another bit of backtracking as US Highway 93 was my route in to, and out from, the casino.

The ride to Cactus Pete's was a smooth, but boring, five hours to cover the 293 miles and I arrived around 5:00 p.m.

*   *   *   *   *   *   *   *   *   *   *

Cactus Pete's Hotel & Casino   *2,370 points*
Anytime
Jackpot, Nevada
Obtain a $1 gambling chip from the casino.
Category: Gambling, organized crime.
This town was born when casinos were shut down in Idaho in 1954 as a result of relentless campaigns against organized crime by a publicity-seeking U.S. senator, Estes Kefauver.
*   *   *   *   *   *   *   *   *   *   *

I needed a chip from the casino, and since the IBR would keep it as proof of the bonus, I wanted to get two in order to have one for posterity. At the cashier's booth I was told that I could only get a one-dollar chip from a table so I found an unused table near the door where the dealer was talking to a security guard. Neither one of them seemed a bit fazed by the fact that I was wearing what appeared to be a black snowmobile suit, had my bright yellow helmet on, and I probably smelled fairly ripe.

I asked for two one-dollar chips and leaned forward to hand two one-dollar bills to the dealer. He drew back a bit and pointed to the table where I then placed the money. He picked up the bills, straightened them out, slid them through his fingers a few times while turning them over and over, and then put them to the side as he picked up two chips.

I put my hand out but he pointed to the table again as he flipped the chips over and over in his hand, ran them through and around each finger, and then finally put them on the table. As I picked them up the guard mentioned to me that the dealer couldn't handle the money directly and I realized that all of the money and chip handling was a show for the ever watchful casino cameras.

I explained that I had never been in a casino before and that I needed the chips for a motorcycle rally. They smiled as if this was an everyday occurrence and I headed back north on Route 93.

The plan now called for me to head to Midvale, Idaho, and then get the last bit of sleep I would have before the end of the rally on Friday. It was 274 miles to Midvale and I would cover those miles in four and a half hours. I planned on sleeping sometime after the bonus and then I would push the last thirty hours to the checkpoint without stopping for anything that wasn't a bonus or fuel stop.

Just after sunset I noticed that my low-beam was not working again. I had swapped the bulb out the night before and the light worked just fine until daybreak. Obviously the bulb was not the faulty part. The only other component in the lighting system was the electronic ballast and I had a spare already mounted and wired-up in the fairing. I stopped at a rest area and only had to shift two electrical plugs and the light was once again working.

Midvale is a small town and I arrived near 10:00 p.m. It was as dark as a small town out west without streetlights can get, which is pretty darned black, and the post office was right next to a bar where I heard loud voices screaming unfriendly things the entire time I was stopped. Even with my helmet on, and earplugs in place, I could hear the yelling and cursing coming from the bar. This was occasionally punctuated by the sound of glass breaking. And I was only there for three minutes.

* * * * * * * * * * *

Post office   *402 points*
Anytime
Midvale, Idaho
Take a photo of the post office.
Category: Sexual solicitation.
Midvale is the birthplace of Sen. Larry Craig (R.ID), famous for adopting a wide stance in a men's room at Minneapolis International Airport. Unfortunately for the senator, his protruding shoe attracted the attention of a vice squad police officer in the adjoining stall. Craig pleaded guilty to sexual solicitation. When the story became widely known, he unsuccessfully sought to withdraw the plea. He decided not to run for re-election in 2008, sparing the voters of Idaho an unending series of jokes on late night television shows.
* * * * * * * * * * *

My goal here was to get my photo and leave before one of the unhappy denizens next door realized that there was a lone biker out front.

Conversely, I was laughing quietly to myself because I was trying to be incognito while standing in the middle of a deserted street taking flash photos of a post office in the middle of the night. .I had to take five pictures of the darkened building in order to get one that I thought would satisfy the IBR scoring staff.

I finally got a photo exposure that showed the information I needed and rode back out of town. Antelope, Oregon, was 300 miles and six hours to the west and I was looking forward to getting a few hours sleep along the way. However, I first had to get back to Interstate 84 and find a hotel. Sounds simple doesn't it?

As I was traveling through Weisner, Idaho, on my way to the interstate my GPS kept me on US Highway 30. Most US Highways are fairly good to excellent roads, sometimes built up to Interstate standards. As I passed through a construction area in the center of town after midnight I followed the signs for US 30 and my GPS didn't argue when I headed out along a riverside road.

After ten miles or so I really started to question the road choice as there were steep drop-offs to the Snake River with no guard rails, missing chunks of pavement, and it seemed as if no maintenance had been done on the road in several generations. There were no streetlights, no houses, not many cross-streets, and the roadside was dirty and run-down. Riding this route at night kept giving me the feeling that I was in some B movie and the living-dead would appear at any moment.

But cars were occasionally passing me in the other direction so I knew that this was a somewhat-used road. I was down to a maximum forty-five miles an hour and had to pay attention to the many unmarked curves and places where gravel had spilled across the pavement, all the while wondering how this road ever got a US Highway designation. On my right I would occasionally get a glimpse through the darkness of the river below, which was easy because there was nothing between me and the water. No trees, guardrails, or even a breakdown-lane. I wondered if the SPOT satellite tracker would work under water.

Then I rounded a curve and saw a highway sign and it said this was "*OLD*" Highway 30 and I realized that I was riding on the old, abandoned, non-maintained, engineered on a goat-trail in the 1800s Highway 30 and that the new and improved Highway 30 was a mile to the East but unreachable from where I rode.

-Day Eleven, Thursday-

I finally linked up to the new US-30 which was a perfectly maintained four lane divided highway and made it to I-84 and found a motel for four hours of sleep around 4:00 a.m. I lurched into my room, set the alarm clock, plugged my phone and camera chargers into the wall, and fell dead asleep on the bed, in my riding suit.

It was Thursday, September 3rd, the last full day of the rally, and for some reason, even though I woke up still wearing my suit, I was feeling better that I had for the past week. Maybe it was because the end was near, the barn was in sight, the light at the end of the tunnel didn't appear to be an oncoming train. You get the picture.

I started out around 7:00 a.m. and had twenty-four hours left to get to the checkpoint in Spokane, Washington. The checkpoint was only 300 miles or five hours away, but as is usual in the IBR the direct route was not the road to travel. I had to make bonuses near Antelope and Corvalis in Oregon as well as Walla Walla and Pasco in Washington. This called for one-thousand miles of riding on the last day of this eleven day rally.

If taken on its own merits, the ride to the Young Life Christian Farm near Antelope was one of the most memorable and enjoyable motorcycle rides that I have ever been on. I traveled along local route 7 to Oregon 19 and through the John Day Fossil Beds National Monument. Roads were perfect and it appeared that the highways had just been paved.

Traffic was light to nonexistent and the speed limits were sixty to sixty-five miles per hour. The motorcycle was a joy to ride along the constantly curving highway and the scenery was incredible. It was mostly desert but not a stinking-hot kind of desert. The landscape was interesting and was made up of medium height rounded buttes and hills. For close to one hundred miles these hills were tinted the green of aged copper.

The ninety-two degree heat was bearable, humidity was low, and the sky was clear. I rode through mountains, valleys, and through bluffs where the highway pass didn't appear till I was right up on it. I was grinning like a madman the entire time and no longer felt the weariness of the last ten days of riding.

But nothing on the IBR is ever straightforward. Riding along on Oregon highway 218 I was looking for what used to be a cult city in the back hills of nowhere that was now a Christian farm. As I approached the turnoff to the farm, Nirvana Drive, from the main road I stopped to talk to two other rally riders who said that they had stopped at the road in question and it led nowhere. They told me that it had a large "no trespassing" sign at its entrance. They had not found a way to the farm and had taken a photo of the sign with their flags and were heading back east to go to another bonus.

I wished them luck and rode on the half mile to Nirvana Drive. The name sounded like what you would name a road going to a cult compound, but there was a five by seven foot brand new sign that said no trespassing in English and Spanish. I took a photo of the sign with my flag in it to prove I was there but felt uneasy about leaving without the points in-hand. This bonus was way too high a point value to hope that this was the right road and that my photo would be acceptable.

I had no reception bars showing on my cell phone so I could not call Lisa Landry but I decided to motor farther down the road before I gave up on the bonus. Less than a mile later I noticed that I had a single bar on the phone and I pulled over to call Lisa. She must have been as busy as a one-armed paperhanger on the last day of the rally but she pointed out that rider Jerry White had visited the farm/compound yesterday.

I told her that I didn't feel good about going past a large "no trespassing" sign into what may be a cult compound. Lisa told me that the person who scouted the bonus would call me back and we hung up.

Roger Van Santen called a minute later and said that I needed to hunt along the main road some more, as he had been to the bonus on his Yamaha FJR just a month ago. He told me that I should look for Cold Camp Road and then Big Muddy Road and I should expect some gravel road riding. I thanked Roger and got back on the highway and not even a hundred feet farther along and around a bend was Cold Camp Road on my left.

I hate gravel roads because the R60 just doesn't handle worth a darn on gravel and neither do I. In the 2007 IBR I had to ride many miles of loose, fresh gravel while on the way to and from Perce Rock during the first leg. The Canadians were building up the roadbed in one area and the gravel was over fifteen feet thick. I know the depth of the fresh gravel because as I was riding along through the construction area in the middle of the night dozens of miles from the nearest village, I realized that my northbound lane started to angle downward with respect to the southbound lane and after a few hundred feet I found myself in a pit that was fifteen feet below the level of the rest of the road.

Back to 2009, Cold Camp Road was three miles of "good" gravel, not too deep, a lot of washboard with lots of rising and falling hills and one or two tight curves. I reminded myself to check the saddlebags when I got to the bonus and again when I made it back to the main road. If the bike held together for that long.

Right on cue I found Big Muddy Road, which to my surprise was a rough asphalt road and to me, anything is better than gravel. This eleven and one half mile road was still rising and falling and turning enough to be technically a challenge but I now saw roadside signs that directed me to the farm and knew that I was on the right route. The road itself was solid and after a while I noticed that it was really clean. No dirt, gravel, or sand was on it.

Just for kicks I told my GPS to re-locate the bonus when I was half way to it on Big Muddy Road. I figured that the GPS would recalculate now that I was on the right road and guide me in. Instead what the electronic monstrosity did was to tell me to go back to the main highway and travel east to Nirvana road and the "no trespassing" sign. It did this even when I was within sight of the water tower at the bonus.

I'm glad that I didn't try the road past the warning sign because it seems that Tom Loftus had done just that the day before. After a few miles of riding he sank his motorcycle into the wash at the side of what used to be a road and had to have a local help him get it free and back out to the main road.

This was desert country, a few small bushes now and then, but emptiness similar to what I saw coming out of Arizona. I kept wondering who would have gone out into this wasteland to do anything. If you look up "the middle of nowhere" in the dictionary it has a photograph of here.

And in the middle of all of this I came around a corner and rode by a man on a street-sweeper cleaning the road. Not a small sweeper or a jury-rigged sweeper mind-you, but a full blown New York style municipal street-sweeper the size of a semi-truck. Even as he waved and smiled I realized that this road has been strikingly clean since I started down it.

Since the sweeper operator didn't shoot at me I now figured that this compound may be safe. I mean, Higdon wouldn't send a rider to an unsafe location would he? In reality I knew that he would not; so as long as I was on the right road I would find the bonus.

After eleven miles of Big Muddy road I rounded another bend and saw a large reservoir, an airfield, and everything around me turned green. As I pulled up to the water tower to take my photo I found another rider who told me that he had ridden cross-country to get this bonus. He rode through pastures, opening and closing cattle gates, and forded streams to get to the water tower.

He said that he was amazed that my R60 made it through all of that and I mentioned that there was a paved road and gravel road back out to the main highway. He stared at me wide-eyed for a three second count and asked if I would lead the way back.

*   *   *   *   *   *   *   *   *   *   *

Young Life Christian farm   *3,874 points*
Daylight hours only
Antelope, Oregon
Take a photo of the water tower.
Category: Biological attack, immigration fraud.
In 1981 Indian con man Bhagwan Shree Rajneesh established a cult city here on a 64,000-acre plot of land, attracting thousands of devoted and determined followers. Almost immediate conflict with neighboring ranchers arose, principally over land use issues. In 1984, seeking to depress voter turnout in a state election, Rajneesh cult members introduced salmonella into ten restaurants in The Dalles, poisoning more than 750 people. To this day it remains the worst biological attack ever experienced on U.S. soil. Rajneesh was deported from the country in 1985. Before his death back in India in 1990, he admitted that his claims to be a God were "a joke."
*   *   *   *   *   *   *   *   *   *   *

This was a cool stop for me. It combined hard-to-find gravel roads and strange roads, mystery, fear, and one heck of a challenge to get to and from. This one bonus emotionally paid for the entire rally. I was standing at an interesting place that I would never have visited if it were not for the Iron Butt Rally. There was a strange-but-true story attached to the bonus that was both frightening and bizarre.

I had read about the biological attack when it was in the news, and even though the cult was long gone, it was an interesting feeling knowing that I was standing where the plan was hatched. I asked the other rider to take a picture of me holding my rally flag, and then entered the bonus information in the rally packet.

I was truly happy that I had not settled for taking a photo of my flag on the "no trespassing" sign back at Nirvana Drive, but had pressed on to the actual bonus. Based on past IBRs, I knew that the riders who did not actually visit the bonus would not receive the points.

As we were leaving a young fellow in a pickup truck drove up and asked us what all of the riders photographing the water tower were up to, and that led to a brief discussion of the rally. He offered us cold water and a place to stop for a bit, but as the clock was ticking away the last minutes of the rally we thanked him and headed out.

The other rider was on a BMW GS, or off-road capable motorcycle, so when we reached the gravel road I let him pass by me since a three year old on a tricycle can go faster than I do on gravel. However, this was a good gravel road and I eventually got up to a whopping forty-five miles an hour. This is painfully slow by most standards of riding but light-speed fast for me, until I had to make a sharp left curve and the bike wanted to go straight. The handlebars started to slam back-and-forth from one steering lock to the other in what is referred to as a tank-slapper and I was headed for the two foot deep ditch on the right side of the road.

At the last possible second I remembered some advice I'd been offered about riding in gravel. I'd been told to stay off of the brakes and give the bike full throttle in order to power through the bad-stuff. I desperately opened the throttle wide and as the R60's fifty horsepower came on-line the front wheel snapped to the straight forward position and I just motored to the left and around that curve. I was now absolutely wide-awake and full of adrenalin. By the way, that curve had a bright yellow motorcycle fender resting at the bottom of the ditch.

When I reached the main highway I stopped and checked my saddlebags and lights and amazingly everything was still attached to the bike and operating. It was time to head west, on a nicely paved road, and when I reached a point where my cell phone worked again I took care of the last call-in bonus and aimed at Corvalis, Oregon.

From Antelope to Corvalis was four hours and 182 miles across Oregon. I rode along US 97 to US 20 and passed near the Three Sisters Mountains and Mt. Washington. The world I was traveling through changed frequently from acres of land that had the appearance of a national park to areas filled with hard-scrabble huts to neighborhoods of high-dollar exclusive housing. The most memorable part was traveling amongst the volcanoes. They just appear out of level land and soar above every other feature.

I was halfway between Antelope and Corvalis when ten and a half days of hard riding caught up with me. The energy I felt when I successfully bagged the Young Life Christian Farm had bled away and I was drained. I just couldn't continue. I pulled over on a dirt forest road in the middle of nowhere and shut down the R60.

I was exhausted and needed to get some rest. I had two more daytime bonuses to get to, and then one more twenty-four hour bonus. After that, all I had to do was ride to the finish. I just had to get my act back together.

I mentally knew that I was in the last half-day of the rally and there were only a few bonuses left. I just couldn't go on. I'd talked with lots of riders who had hit the wall within sight of the end of the rally. It's fairly common. I'd done just that in 2007 on day nine. It was one thing to know, to think, that all I had to do was cover a few hundred more miles. It was an entirely different matter to get up the "oomph" to do it.

I sat down in the dirt next to the BMW and ate a protein bar, a package of chocolate chip cookies, and drank a warm bottle of "Iced Tea" I had bought that morning. I knew from experience that it would take a short while before I would feel the effect of the food, so I set the alarm clock for a half hour and shut my eyes.

I don't think that I really fell asleep, but when the alarm sounded off I felt refreshed. I called Susie to tell her where I was and just hear her cheer me on, and then cranked up the bike and pushed west. I got to the bonus in Corvalis just after 3:00 p.m.

* * * * * * * * * * *

Pleasure Acres Thoroughbred Farm *3,576 points*
Anytime
Corvallis, Oregon

Take a photo of the Pleasure Acres sign opposite mile marker 1.

Category: Animal abuse.

In June 2007 a teenage boy — who else? — was caught on closed circuit TV having sex with a horse in a barn near here. This farm isn't where the actual crime took place, but it should have been.

*   *   *   *   *   *   *   *   *   *   *

The next bonus on the plan was three hundred miles to the northeast and was a daylight only bonus. The problem was that the five hour trip would put me at the bonus right at sunset and any delay meant I would miss out on 758 points. Most of the route was on I-5 and I-84 and should have been a breeze to ride so I headed out.

As I approached Portland I had to decide whether to go around the city or through it. Truckers on the CB told me that there were no problems on the by-pass so that is the route I took. Things can change fast on a modern highway and I watched the rally clock tick down as traffic came to a standstill just south of the city. Word on the CB was that this was simply the normal traffic mess for Portland and it's not due to any accident or other problem. So much for taking advice from truckers.

After taking thirty minutes to travel five miles the traffic abruptly cleared and I was heading east on I-84, which parallels the Columbia river. I was blown away by the Columbia. Just the sheer size puts most rivers I've seen to shame. It travels through solid rock cliffs and steep bluffs and it's clear to see that even though it is impressive now, it was once considerably more massive.

Part of my fascination with the Columbia is its history. During the last ice age, 15,000 years ago, glaciers formed an ice-dam which closed off the drainage from a large part of Montana and Idaho and this formed a large lake called Glacial Lake Missoula that was the size of lakes Erie and Superior combined. The lake was centered in Montana and in places it was over 2,000 feet deep.

Roughly every one hundred years the waters of the lake would finally force the glacial ice-dam to float and break apart and this would unleash a flood of an inconceivable size as the lake drained through the route I was following along the Columbia River basin to the Pacific.

It is estimated that Glacial Lake Missoula would drain in just two weeks' time and for that period ten times more water flowed through the Columbia River channel than all of the rivers in the world combined. Water levels at what is now Portland, Oregon, were over four hundred feet deep. This drainage of the lake occurred at least forty times over 2,000 years. If a rider pays attention traveling along the Columbia they can see the scouring of the bedrock and the sites of ancient waterfalls and gorges all the way from the Pacific to Montana.

As I rode along, passing monumental dams and massive bridges, there was little time for admiring the scenery because I was always checking the clock, watching the total average speed display, and the ETA readout for the Whitman bonus. I also noted a new yellow wildlife caution sign which had a silhouette of a bighorn sheep.

It was a long ride and a lot could go wrong, or right. I encountered light traffic and good roads through I-82, and then just as I was approaching US Highway 12, which would take me to the bonus, I realized that I would have to make a fuel stop, which would eat up some time. I had no time to spare.

Even though I carry five extra gallons of gas I hate to stretch miles to the limits for fear of running out where no fuel is available. There are innumerable tales of IBR riders who woulda, coulda, shoulda, but didn't get gas when they could have and ended up losing hours due to running out of fuel. My GPS contains listings of gas stations, motels, hotels, and restaurants so I could look ahead to find fuel, lodging, or food. I had enough fuel to make the bonus but the gas station listings on my GPS indicated that it might be beyond my range to get to the next fuel after the bonus.

As I leaned right and pulled off the Interstate I was mentally wound up about the time element and getting these points, but I found a gas station at the foot of the ramp. It had brand new pay-at-the-pump gas dispensers and it gave me a good receipt. I was in and out in just two and a half minutes and then rapidly moving east toward Walla Walla.

Six miles from the bonus it was just a few minutes till sunset and it gets dark in a hurry around here, so I stopped in Touchet at a filling station and got a few gallons of gas in order to have a good receipt to prove I was in the area near sunset; now all I needed was the photo.

*   *   *   *   *   *   *   *   *   *   *

Whitman Mission National Historic Site *758 points*
Daylight hours only
Walla Walla, Washington
Take a photo of the memorial shaft. It is at the end of a 200-yard paved path at the top of a hill.
Category: Indian massacre.
On 11/29/1847 missionary Marcus Whitman, his wife, and twelve others were slain by Cayuse Indians.
*   *   *   *   *   *   *   *   *   *   *

How hard could it be? Find the paved path, climb the hill, and take the photo. As the light faded I circled the point where the path should be and couldn't find a hill.

I walked along a back road behind the site and found a housing development. I wandered around the parking lot and still didn't see the hill. It was getting darker and I was getting bushed. It was easy to feel enthusiastic about bonus hunting when I was successful at it. It was fatiguing when I was following the directions and couldn't figure out where the path was. So for the fourth and final time this rally I called Lisa. She handed the phone to Dale Wilson who had scouted the bonus for the rally.

Dale asked me where I was standing and I told him I was in front of the visitor's center. He told me to put the flashlight in my right hand. Not my left hand, my right hand, and look at the side door of the building. I told him I had done as he ordered and he said "walk forward" and then while he was mumbling something about this being a daylight bonus he hung up. Two steps later I was on the path and climbing the hill.

As I walked up the hill in the dark at the deserted Historic Site I heard the voices of two men coming down the path toward me and I asked into the darkness just how far it was to the memorial. One voice told me that it's just a few hundred feet and another said that I couldn't miss it at the top. I thanked them and as they walked by me in what little light was left in the sky I noticed that one of them was wearing a skirt and blouse. One more bit to remember on this rally.

I found the memorial shaft at the top of the hill and took my bonus photo using the flash. I knew that based on the lack of light in the sky I needed to get another receipt to prove that I made the one hour after sunset grace period, so I hustled back to the same gas station I'd just visited but now I was not too worried about time. I fueled the R60 for the last time this rally and grabbed a celebratory crème-filled strawberry snowball cake. I then relaxed for two minutes while I watched the stars start to appear in the night sky.

I only had one more "anytime" bonus one hour or fifty-six miles north and then it was on to the checkpoint in Spokane. I had ten hours till the checkpoint window opened, only had to cover two hundred miles to get there, and it was all via Interstate highways. I was starting to feel rejuvenated.

*   *   *   *   *   *   *   *   *   *   *

ZZ Streetrods sign   *1,079 points*
Anytime
Pasco, Washington
Take a photo of the ZZ Streetrods sign.
Category: False police report.
Daniel Kuch told police that he had been wounded in a drive-by shooting near here. It was subsequently revealed that the Iraq war veteran had a friend shoot him in the shoulder so that Kuch could get some time off of work and avoid an upcoming drug test.
*   *   *   *   *   *   *   *   *   *   *

It was good to end the rally at a bonus that made me smile instead of at a somber or dreadful one. On the lonely road riding in to this bonus I was passed by four separate riders coming out, and when I arrived at the sign I met a rider who was just about at the end of his rope. He had suffered from back pain for days, couldn't sleep, and could not wait to call the rally "over." On the other hand, I was bubbling with enthusiasm that we were within sight of the finish.

After securing the bonus and heading to the checkpoint I was thinking of trying for one last bonus that was only open from 5:00 to 7:00 a.m. at a restaurant seventy-five miles from the finish.

*   *   *   *   *   *   *   *   *   *   *

Zip's Drive In   *2,327 points*
Friday, September 4
5:00 a.m. – 7:00 a.m.
Sandpoint, Idaho
Enjoy something to eat or drink here and obtain a receipt.
Category: Espionage, prison escape.
Christopher Boyce (the "Falcon" of the true-crime book <u>The Falcon and the Snowman</u>) frequented a nearby Sandpoint restaurant while on the run after escaping from a federal prison in Lompoc, California in January 1980. Since the actual restaurant doesn't open early enough, we're giving the business to IBR veteran Michael Boge.

*   *   *   *   *   *   *   *   *   *   *

I figured that I could easily be at the Drive-In at 5:00 a.m., and then return to the hotel just before the checkpoint opened and the penalty clock started ticking. I had been thinking about this route all day long and just couldn't decide what to do. While it seemed like these would be relatively easy points to get, I was tired.

In the back of my mind I knew that I still had over 2,650 miles to ride after the rally in order to get home. The wear and tear of the past eleven days was starting to drag at me and I needed to get some decent rest. Maybe a whole eight hours of sleep.

I thought about this all the way to the checkpoint and finally realized that I was worn out, and the 2,327 points wouldn't affect my success in the rally. I was happy with the rally, the BMW, and just needed to finish.

9 Finished (finally!)

-The Finish, Friday-

So, a little before 1:00 a.m., I pulled into the hotel parking lot and called an end to my Iron Butt Rally. As I unloaded the bike Vicky Johnston, an IBR veteran, walked up and told me that she was the official greeting committee and it's good to see me at the checkpoint safe and sound.

The last time I had seen Vicky was at the Perce Rock bonus in Northern Quebec during the first leg of the 2007 IBR. This was the largest bonus of the leg and to score it the rider had to get to Perce Rock at low tide to be able to walk to the rock for the bonus photo. There was only one four-hour window for low tide based on the mileage, time, and the length of the rally leg.

I was just leaving the R60 to wade across the ocean floor as Vicky was walking back to her bike. She mentioned that the tide was still going out and was low enough to wade and that I was on the right path. It was another of those chance encounters by riders thousands of miles and days into the rally. Spending a moment talking with another rally rider, and an IBR veteran, reassured me that my plan for the first leg was sound.

In Spokane, Vicky asked about my rally and I told her that my one goal for the entire ride was to cross the finish line grinning, which I certainly had. My rally was a success.

Eleven days and still smiling

I checked into the hotel and spent the next thirty minutes getting my rally pack ready for scoring. I checked and double checked my receipts, bonus sheets, and photos. I made sure that I had crossed every "t" and dotted every single "i" so I would not lose any points at the scoring table. I cross checked everything and then went to sleep for a few hours until early scoring opened up at 4:00 a.m.

You would think by this time that everything IBR was over. I just had to get scored, attend the finishing banquet, and then head home. You would be wrong, as there are still tales to tell and the fat lady had not yet shown up to sing.

At 4:00 a.m. on Friday the 4th my alarm went off just seconds after Vicky Johnston called to make sure I didn't oversleep scoring.   I felt as if I was ready for anything as I headed in to the scoring room clutching my bag of materials.

Roger Van Santen was my scorer and he asked if I was ready to start the process and I said "Sure." This was "it". This was the culmination of all of the planning, practicing, dreaming, training, and spending.   I was confident that I had exceeded the requirements to be a finisher and just had the formality of final-scoring to go.

The first things Roger looked over were my gas receipts and he compared them to what I'd entered on my gas-log.   On the third receipt he said that I had entered an eight on my log, whereas I should have entered a zero.

I broke out in a cold sweat as I assured him that the number he was looking at on the computer generated receipt was an eight and not a zero with a bar through the center. To my absolute freaking horror Roger then pulled out a magnifying glass. Not a little pocket magnifying glass, but a large round glass with a large black handle. The IBR folk take scoring seriously.

The rules for scoring have been explained again and again to the riders. No matter what happens, the rider must not get upset or be disrespectful to the scoring staff. The staff volunteers their time and they are tasked with scoring on a black and white basis. The bonus meets all requirements exactly or it is denied. Being rude to a scorer is grounds for disqualification from the rally. I began to seriously wonder if it would be considered disrespectful if I became violently ill.

Roger held the receipt up to the light as he looked at it with the magnifying glass like Sherlock Holmes studying a fragment of bone and said "No, look at this eight here and this zero over here and you can see that there is a slight angle to the zero cross bar but no angle at all on the crossbar on the eight." I looked through the magnifying glass and he was right. By a few ten-thousandths of an inch there was a difference. It was definitely a zero when studied on the subatomic level and one hundred and twenty-five points disappeared in a mist of cheap dot-matrix ink.

I sat back as Roger continued through the rest of the rally pack. I was nauseous and my confidence in finishing the rally evaporated. I began to feel the weariness that this eleven day motorcycle rally had stamped on my soul. My thoughts crowded around the focus of how my point cushion for finishing could disappear if I'd made another error or if the timing on a bonus was ruled incorrect.

I was second-guessing my dropping the Zip's Drive-In bonus from the route and was mentally beating myself up for fouling up the first call-in bonus on the second leg. I began dreading another DNF due to some unforeseen and unimagined error. My mind was a churning mass of mush and I was feeling decidedly queasy. I guess I can try again in 2011.

But everything else was fine and I ended up with 45,706 points for the leg after riding over 3,800 miles. I started the leg 450 points behind the number needed to be a finisher but ended with a 5,256 point cushion and finally "finished" the Iron Butt Rally on the R60.

On my way out of the scoring room one of the rally veterans, Tobie Stevens, walked up and shook my hand. As he was doing this he said in a low, half-crazed, melodramatic voice "You're one of us now." He cackled and walked away.

I headed to the hotel restaurant and had my first sit-down meal in eleven days. It is impossible to explain how it feels to place an order for food and not have to worry about how long it is taking to prepare. Then there is the remarkable feeling of eating, at a table, without thinking about what the meal is costing in terms of miles or sleep.

As I ate I talked with other riders about what had gone on over the course of the rally. Some stories were good and some were bad.

I found out that one of our riders, Davo Jones, had hit a deer that very morning and was in the hospital. No one knew his condition but the word had circulated that he was not wearing his helmet when he went down. Wearing a helmet is mandatory on the rally. It is not a point that a rider can argue or find a workaround. Each rider is videotaped at the start of the rally agreeing to the helmet rule, so why Davo may not have been wearing his was a mystery. We all were hoping for good news as the day passed.

I learned that neither of the two Suzuki RE-5 motorcycles in the hopeless class had finished. The first had suffered a catastrophic engine failure on day one, and the other had broken down in Iowa on day four. Both riders found other motorcycles to continue the rally. One of them qualified as a finisher. The last hopeless Class rider on a 1982 Honda GL1100 did not finish.

I had planned to be near the checkpoint computer to watch the other riders arrive, but even as riders were pulling up to the hotel the strain of the last eleven days of riding hit me and I headed back to my room for eight hours of real sleep. I checked in with Susie, who was elated that I finished. She has been unrelenting over the years in her support for my strange hobby and I couldn't have made it through the rally without her constant love and understanding. I then hit the hay without setting the alarm or putting a sticky note on the clock.

Around 2:00 p.m. I awoke, put on clean clothes, and got ready to check the valves on the BMW and perform an oil and filter change prior to returning to North Carolina the next morning.

While I was sleeping I had a few dreams involving a train. A check of my cell phone, which has an old steam-locomotive whistle for a ringtone, cleared that mystery up. Tim Lasley, a really good friend for over thirty years and my Fire Chief at Vienna Volunteer Fire Department in North Carolina, had been following my SPOT track on the internet. Tim is always enthusiastic and called to congratulate me on finishing the rally. Talking with him made me realize that the wretched weight of the monkey-on-my-back that I've carried since the DNF in 2007 had disappeared.

The afternoon after the rally was a time to wind down. H. Marc Lewis, another IBR veteran and a local resident, had volunteered to bring an oil container to the hotel so I could change the oil and filter on the R60. One exhaust valve was one, one-thousandth of an inch too tight which is well within accepted limits and I would normally ignore it, but I set the proper clearance since I was staring at the valve-train anyway. Nothing else on the bike needed attention. Not a single thing.

The R60 had run a great rally and never hiccupped. Losing the saddlebag was a problem with the home-engineered mount and having a thirty-three year old weld break was grim but not remarkable. I did have lots of folks make the joke that you would think BMW would design their hardware better than they did. After all it only lasted thirty-three years and 523,000 miles.

The work that Nathan and Dean did at Boxerworks prior to the rally was just what the bike needed. In all seriousness, the extra ten horsepower that I gained going from a 600cc to a 750cc engine did the trick. I was able to go as fast as I wanted and had the torque that was missing in the 2007 rally to make mountain roads a pleasure. I averaged forty-three miles per gallon through the rally, which was remarkable considering that I was near full-throttle for nineteen hours each day.

In the 116 degree heat outside of Santa Ana the engine never missed a beat and I used about one quart of oil every 1,000 miles, which is fine on this old a motorcycle. I was plumb tickled with the bike.

Actually I was pleased beyond belief with the whole rally. Granted, trying to find a welder in Mississippi and staring at the broken saddlebag in Texas weren't fun, but they were problems that were solved fairly quickly and I felt satisfaction that they were the only mishaps during the eleven day event.

At 5:30 Friday evening everyone gathered for the finishing banquet. I was relieved and excited at the same time. I had finished and I really didn't care what place I had finished in. At least that's what I said out loud. In reality I was pretty interested in how well the R60 and I had done in comparison with the rest of the field.

Dinner was short and every rider had stories to tell of what they had overcome in terms of riding conditions, weather, weariness, illness, and adventure. The camaraderie was intense as almost everyone at my table was a veteran of the IBR. We had all faced similar challenges and threats in completing the eleven day event and fully understood the victory or angst that accompanied each story. I was just starting to understand that I had finally become a full-fledged member of a very eccentric group of riders and I was feeling exceptionally good about that.

When Bob Higdon took the podium to start the awards ceremony we learned that thirty-one of the one-hundred and one riders had failed to finish due to accident, breakdown, or other reasons. He then read off the names and points of the finishers starting with seventieth place and each rider arose to a round of well-earned applause as they walked to the podium to receive their finisher's plaque.

When he got to 60th place and read my name he added that I had finished with over 523,000 miles on the R60 and there was a standing ovation that lasted until I got back to my seat. This reaction to my finish from this group of hard-riders stunned me. I shook Bob's hand and Mike Kneebone's hand as I received my plaque and license plate-back which states "*Iron Butt Rally 11 Days 11,000 miles*".

I had officially covered 10,554 miles in the eleven days and had done it on a motorcycle that was a third of a century old and a half-million miles worn. My final score was 81,106 points. I was also realizing that this rally had been fun. Other than the glitches with the side-stand and saddlebag I had a good time. Sure, I was relentlessly weary at times, but in 2007 there were several times each day that I wondered why I was doing what I was doing, and that sense of despair never happened during this rally. Not once!

Instead of cursing the rain or the traffic or the clock or the heat or the distance, I had looked at these things as challenges and I was digging the ride. It was fun. I certainly wasn't as good at figuring out the bonus puzzle as the fifty-nine riders who finished ahead of me, but I did remarkably better than I had in 2007. I was a happy camper!

The top ten riders:

	Rider	Leg 3	Total
1	Jim Owen	12706	139833
2	Jeff Earls	12153	136090
3	Eric Jewell	12090	130388
4	Chris Sakala	12238	126481
5	Greg Marbach	11931	122021
6	Mike Hutsal	11321	117843
7	Rick Miller	11388	114326
8	Bob Lilly	12268	111836
9	Ken Meese	11047	111129
10	Peter Behm	11891	109350

10 It Ain't Over Till.......

After the banquet I confirmed with Bill Thweatt that he and I would leave the next morning, Saturday, at 5:30, for North Carolina. Bill lived in Charlotte just a few miles down the road from me and we both had to be at work on the Tuesday morning after Labor Day, so we would ride back together.

The last time I rode any distance with other motorcyclists was in 1978 and I found that trying to pace myself with a group just didn't work. Deciding when to get gas, when to eat, when to pee, when to stop for the day, what to stop and look at, and how long to spend at each stop never worked out right. My riding habits didn't sync with theirs. It all drove me to frustration and I haven't ridden with anyone since. So the idea of riding 2,655 miles in two days with another rider would be an entertaining experience to say the least.

At 5:30 a.m. we left the hotel parking lot and stopped at a gas station a few blocks away. The station was closed, but the pumps were powered up and we filled up at different islands. After I put the nozzle back on the pump I realized that the printer on the pump was out of paper and I wasn't going to get a receipt. I started fussing loudly about the damned receipt and having to take a picture and document the station. I was irate and cussing like a sailor as in a split second I had tripped from happy-go-lucky to pissed-off.

Then, from the other gas island I heard Bill yell "The rally is over." "It's over." "You - don't - need - a - receipt." He was laughing so hard he could barely get the words out.

He was right of course. But, after years of training, setting a regular routine for fueling, and just ending the IBR where a receipt can make or break you, it is truly hard to return to the everyday. I grinned at Bill, climbed on the R60, and we headed east.

The two days passed quickly. We would ride four hundred miles, fuel up, and eat a quick breakfast. Four hundred miles fuel up and take a bathroom break. Four hundred miles fuel up and eat a quick dinner and then another hundred miles to find a motel for four hours of sleep. We talked on the CB occasionally to compare notes on our routing or on the rally just passed.

Susie called and told me on the first day of the return ride that Davo Jones had died from his injuries and after I passed this on to Bill it led to a hundred miles or so of silence. I had met Davo in Spartanburg and talked with him at the other checkpoints. Davo was the founder of FarRiders.com, which was set up to encourage safe long-distance motorcycle riding in Australia. He had proven himself to be a darned good rider and was riding well throughout this IBR.

Law enforcement reports from the crash scene say that he was traveling less than forty-five miles an hour, and his motorcycle helmet was securely fastened to the rear rack on his bike. His passing, after hitting a deer only eighty miles from the finish of the rally, was a stone-sobering moment for everyone who knew him.

Two other parts of this ride home come to mind. At one point Bill and I decided to take a detour off of the Interstate in order to save eighty miles. It only took us a few seconds while we rode to compare notes and decide to change our route. The detour involved two states and six hours of riding. We were both chuckling about our approach to routing and riding where a six hour detour was just a small adjustment. It made perfect sense to us to do it because we were riding for nineteen hours that day anyway.

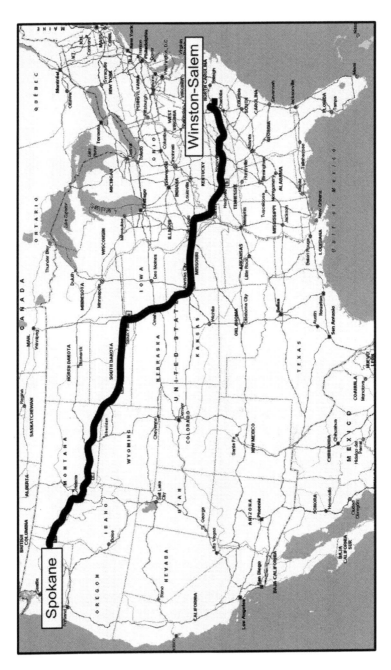

Two days to get back home

The other moment was at a rest stop in Tennessee when a man wandered over as we were closing up our riding suits for a large storm ahead. The sky to the south was pitch black, the wind was picking up, the NEXRAD weather-radar showed lots of red and orange areas, and we could hear the lightning strikes.

The gentleman asked where we were from and Bill told him North Carolina and that we were on our way home. I added a bit about the IBR and Bill said that we had done thirteen thousand miles in the last fourteen days and were only five hundred miles from home, and we would get there the next morning. The gentleman let us know through body language and his voiced disbelief that he knew we were lying through our teeth. He was convinced that no one could cover anywhere near the amount of miles we were claiming in just fourteen days.

As the stranger turned his back and stalked away Bill looked at me and grinned as he said "Some folks just don't get it." We saddled up and rode off into two hours of severe thundershowers as if it was just another easy day-ride. Actually, it was just that.

Monday morning just after dawn Bill and I split up in Asheville, North Carolina. He headed south to Charlotte and I motored east toward home. Our riding styles had matched up better than I could have imagined. The fuel range of our motorcycles was the same and our need to stop worked out just fine. I had truly enjoyed the company.

I was only a few hours from home and riding on familiar roads. I pulled into my driveway after 13,400 miles and fourteen days feeling good.

Getting over the rally took time. Just like the angst I felt when I didn't get a receipt for gas in Spokane, I had tuned myself for the rally and the training took quite a while to wear off. It was over a month before I stopped waking up in the middle of the night in a panic thinking that I had overslept and needed to get to a bonus.

Several times I was out of bed and half-dressed before I realized that Susie was telling me that "The rally is over and you are home." Sometimes she had to say it a few times because I was busy dressing, trying to remember where I was and where I had to be all at the same time. Then I would lay back down to go to sleep again while still convincing myself that I really was at home and not having a dream during the rally.

I worried about everyday things such as how long it took me to eat lunch since I was used to a three-minute-meal. Sitting in a restaurant to eat was a long luxury that made me flat-out nervous. It was December before life returned to normal.

I gather that it is difficult for a lot of folks to understand why I would ride in something like the Iron Butt Rally. When I talk about the rally some say that they like to ride motorcycles too, but... Or that they like to travel to new places too, but... Or that the idea of having a relatively unplanned adventure is great, but...

For me the IBR was a combination of all of the things that I enjoy and there were no "buts" (pun intended). I went to places that I didn't even suspect existed just for the sake of getting there. I saw new parts of the country, met lots of different people, and pushed my limits for endurance riding well past any point I'd ever considered to be achievable.

Of the three hundred and ten million people in the Unites States, approximately seven million ride motorcycles. A handful of those ride long-distances and just a smattering of these riders has ever heard of the Iron Butt Rally. Even fewer people care about the IBR and actually follow the rally news. In other words, riders don't ride this rally for fame or fortune and it certainly isn't a relaxing hobby.

I have ridden the IBR twice and the same reasons keep coming to mind. I enjoy the mental and physical challenge of safely riding the distance and overcoming the obstacles to finish. I enjoy the fellowship of a group of riders who have the same defective gene as I do and are enthusiastic about the same type of endless riding that I am. Finally, the Iron Butt Rally was a grand adventure and any adventures at all are few and far between in the modern world. All of this combines to leave me with a grin every time I think about this Iron Butt Rally.

My finishing position was adjusted the day after the rally to 59th place. Those who complete the rally are awarded a new Iron Butt Association membership number based on their addition to the list of rally finishers. My membership number changed from 15,822 to 397. I am unreasonably proud of having that three digit number.

A comparison that comes up when explaining the IBR is that more people have climbed to the top of Mount Everest in a single year than have finished the Iron Butt Rally in its entire history. Four hundred and twenty-three climbers made it to the summit of Mount Everest in 2009. Four hundred and three riders have finished the IBR since its inception in 1984.

The first day I was at work after the rally I was talking about the ride to several folks and one asked me how I had done. I told him that I had finished. He asked where I had finished in the standings and I said 59th to which he exclaimed "You spent all of that money and time just to finish 59th?"

I was going to explain that a person climbing Everest didn't care whether they were the first person at the summit that season or the last as they were standing on the top of the world. I was going to emphasize the grand adventure I had been on. I was going to speak to the challenge of covering eleven thousand miles in eleven days.

Instead, I just looked at him, grinned, and said "Yes." Bill Thweatt was correct when he said "Some people just don't get it!"

FINIS - The Fat-Lady Sings

A few months after I got back from the IBR I did something that I never thought I would do. I had a tattoo put on my left forearm to commemorate my finishing the rally.

For fifty-seven years I had resisted tattoos because I never knew of anything that I would want permanently displayed on my body. Finishing the World's Toughest Motorcycle Competition gave me a reason to proudly highlight the accomplishment.

Errata

Bonus information and artwork from the Iron Butt Association website was used with permission of the Iron Butt Association.

The phrases "World's Toughest Motorcycle Riders", Iron Butt Association, Iron Butt Rally, Saddlesore, Bun Burner, 100CCC, and the globe logo are registered trademarks of the Iron Butt Association.

Information on the **Iron Butt Magazine** can be obtained by writing to:
Iron Butt Association, PO Box 4223, Lisle, IL 60532

The author's website with more information on the 2007 IBR and the R60/6 is http://rappoport.ws/   The site is hosted courtesy of Tim and Vickey Sailer

Information about the Iron Butt Association is at
http://ironbutt.com/about/default.cfm

Information about the 2009 Iron Butt Rally is at
http://www.ironbuttrally.com/IBR/2009.cfm

Information on the **Hard Miles 2** video is at
http://www.apgvideo.com/ironbuttrally/faq/

Additional Bits-And-Pieces

The motorcycle is a 1976 BMW R60/6
It was bought new in 1976 by the author.

Modifications include:

-Engine displacement has been increased to 750cc.
-The original front drum brake was changed to twin Brembo disc brakes.
-The transmission and final drive were rebuilt.
All of this was done at Boxerworks in Watkinsville, Georgia.
Many thanks for exceptional help with parts, service, advice, and harassment from Nathan and Dean.
http://www.Boxerworks-service.com/
-Len Hoffman of Hoffman Automotive Machine Shop in Athens, Georgia, provided expert work on the valve train.
- A high-output Omega charging system, Nippo Denso starter, and LED taillight from Motorrad Elektric.
http://www.motoelekt.com/
-The Hannigan fairing was mounted with help from Jerry and Barbara Heil, owners of Hannigan Motorcycle Fairings.
www.hanniganmotorcyclefairings.com
-A set of Kawasaki 1000 police saddlebags were donated by "Chicken" Larry Sexton.
-A Bridgestone tire was donated courtesy of Ted Porter at www.beemershop.com/
-A custom saddle by Rocky Mayer did an excellent job.
-I used a SPOT, first generation, satellite tracker and Spotwalla.com to keep the family aware of where I was.
-The stock 5.8 gallon fuel tank was augmented with a Jaz 5 gallon fuel cell on a custom built rack. The system was a gravity feed to the carburetors.

-The stock H-4 Headlight was converted to an 'always on' HID low beam lamp (4300 degree Kelvin).
-A Boyer electronic ignition system was used.
-The engine was double-plugged in 1978 to reduce 'ping'.
-Two Phillips HID driving lamps (4300 Kelvin) were used as high beams.
-Two Hella H-3 fog lamps augmented the low beam.
-A Pelican cargo case was used to house the laptop.
-The R60 was shod with Avon RoadRider tires.
-There was a handlebar mount CB with cell phone, GPS, and music integration.
-Navigation was via two Garmin GPSmap 478 units.
-Comfort and survival was through use of LD Comfort underwear. Long sleeve top and shorts. (I will wear long tights instead of shorts on future rides).

Other equipment included;
-First Gear TGP riding suit.
-Nolan N-102 helmet.
-Warm N Safe electric jacket.
-Aerostitch Vegan hot weather gloves.
-Aerostitch TL Tec blue fleece pants.
-Socks by Techsocks. (the knee-length worked well, the calf-length would work better).

Spare Parts

It may seem like a lot, but it all fit neatly in the bike.

In the left saddlebag

Tire pump	Gear deodorizer
Temperature controllers	Head lamp
Shorts	Carrier bag
Shirt	Safety glasses
Socks	Memory cards
Digital voltmeter	Spare camera
Zip-ties	Tire gauge
Earbuds	Lightweight gloves
Towel	Charging rotor
Quart of oil	Alarms
Lithium batteries	Oil funnels
Wet-ones	Recording tapes

In the right saddlebag

Clutch cable	Spark plug caps
Throttle cable	Diode board
Speedometer cable	Front tube
Spark plug wire	Rear tube
Fuel line	Cables kit bag
Fuel quick-connect	Bite valves
Ignition module	GPS
Bead breaker	Dial caliper
Jumper cables	Eye and nose drops
HID ballast	H-3 bulbs
Valve cover gaskets	Ignition coil
Fuses	Epoxy roll
Ignition switch	JB weld epoxy
Electric wire	Alligator clips

Under the seat	Red parts bag
Oil cover gasket	Throwout bearing
Headlight relay	Gasket kit
Petcock nipples	Side-stand spring
Petcock screens	Fairing hardware
Instrument bulbs	Clutch pivot pin
Brush springs	Oil sender
Wheel bearings	Carb springs
Bearing spacers	Fuel filters
Points	Crimp connectors
Rear wheel seals	Carb rebuild kit
Gas kits	Timing cover gasket
Rotor brushes	Relay
Voltage regulator	Drain plugs

In the trunk - Blue bag	
Spare cables	iPod cable
Inverter	Photo cable
Earbud accessories	GPS cable
120 v GPS charger	USB cable
120 v GPS charger/speaker	

Medical bag

In the fairing

Front storage compartment	
Wiring diagrams	Spark plug caps
BMW anonymous book	Aluminum blanket
XL glove covers	HID Bulb
Thermals .	Duct tape
Oil filter	Large Zip ties
Smartwool gloves	Map markers

Right pocket

Paper maps for 49 states
Gray pants

Left pocket

First aid kit

Tie-straps

Rags

Black instrument cover

Phone rain cover

Outside rear case

Motorcycle cover

Flip flops

Umbrella

WD-40

One quart of oil